Through Year with Hafiz

Selection of the Most Common
Verses of Hafiz

In Farsi with
English translation

Translated By:
Henry Wilberforce Clarke

Created by:
Hamid Eslamian

Through the Year with Hafiz

Published by Persian Learning Center

Web: www.persianbell.com

Email: info@persianbell.com

Copyright © 2024

Persian Learning Center.

All rights reserved. No part of this publication may be reproduced, stored in a retrieval system, or transmitted in any form or by any means, electronic, mechanical, photocopying, recording, scanning, or otherwise, except as permitted under Section 107 or 108 of the 1976 United States Copyright Ac, without permission of the author.

All inquiries should be addressed to the Persian Learning Center.

ISBN: 978-1-63620-913-5

Join a Year of Spiritual Delights with Hafiz

Unfold your soul with the captivating poetry of Hafiz. Celebrated for his passionate odes to love, mystical rapture, and the joyous dance of existence, Hafiz offers profound insights alongside his soulful verses.

This anthology features his most beloved poems, carefully selected from the 'Divan of hafiz.' They are organized according to the four seasons of the solar year—spring, summer, autumn, and winter—aligned with the natural world's cycle (2025). It offers 365 days of soulful engagement with Hafiz's wisdom.

This bilingual book is excellent for:
Personal growth: Enhance your spiritual journey with Hafiz's profound insights.
Poetry enthusiasts: Relish the lyrical beauty of Hafiz's words, available in both the original and translated forms.
Those with busy lives: Discover quick moments of inspiration and contemplation.
Gift-givers: Offer the life-altering experience of Hafiz's poetry to loved ones.

Allow Hafiz to lead you through the varying seasons of life, drawing inspiration from nature and the inner divine flame.

www.prersianbell.com

... So Much More Online!

- ✓ FREE Farsi Lessons
- ✓ More Farsi Learning Books!
- ✓ Persian Lessons
- ✓ Online Farsi Tutors

For a PDF Version of This Book

Email: info@persianbell.com

Contents

فصل بهار (Spring) 7

فروردین 7
April 7

اردیبهشت 19
May 19

خرداد 31
June 31

فصل تابستان (Summer) 43

تیر 43
July 43

مرداد 55
August 55

شهریور 67
September 67

فصل پاییز (Autumn) 79

مهر 79
October 79

آبان 90
November 90

آذر 101
December 101

فصل زمستان (Winter) 113

دی 113
January 113

بهمن 124
February 124

اسفند 135
March 135

فصل بهار
(Spring)

فروردین
April

۱ فروردین - March 21

ز کوی یار می‌آید نسیم باد نوروزی
From the street of the friend (the perfect murshid) came the fragrant breeze of the nau-ruz (guidance in the Path to God)

از این باد ار مدد خواهی چراغ دل برافروزی
From this breeze, if thou desire aid, the lamp of the heart, thou mayest kindle.

چو گل گر خرده‌ای داری خدا را صرف عشرت کن
If, like the red rose, a particle of (red gold) thou hast, for God's sake, expend it in pleasure

که قارون را غلط‌ها داد سودای زراندوزی
For caused Karun's errors, the passion for gold-gathering.

۲ فروردین - March 22

گلبن عیش می‌دمد ساقی گلعذار کو
Pleasure's rose-bush blossometh the Saki, rose of cheek, where

باد بهار می‌وزد باده خوشگوار کو
Bloweth the spring breeze the pleasant tasting wine, where

هر گل نو ز گلرخی یاد همی کند ولی
Recollection of one rose of cheek (the beloved) keepeth giving every fresh rose But,

گوش سخن شنو کجا دیده اعتبار کو
The ear, speech (of counsel) hearing where The eye of caution (to see) where

۳ فروردین - March 23

شکر آن را که دگربار رسیدی به بهار
For thanks for that, that again to spring thou hast reached,

بیخ نیکی بنشان و ره تحقیق بجوی
The root of goodness, plant; (the rose of the grace of God smell)

دو نصیحت کنمت بشنو و صد گنج ببر
Thee, two counsels I make, Hear; and a hundred treasures bear away:

از در عیش درآ و به ره عیب مپوی
By the door of pleasure, enter in the path of defect, do not strive.

March 24 - ۴ فروردین

نوبهار است در آن کوش که خوشدل باشی
'Tis the fresh spring. In this strive that joyous of heart thou mayst be
که بسی گل بدمد باز و تو در گل باشی
For, again, blossometh many arose when in the clay (of the grave) thou shall be.

من نگویم که کنون با که نشین و چه بنوش
I say not now, with whom, sit what drink
که تو خود دانی اگر زیرک و عاقل باشی
For thou knowest, if wise and learned thou be

March 25 - ۵ فروردین

ساقیا سایه ابر است و بهار و لب جوی
O Saki[1] tis the shade of the cloud, and spring, and the stream-bank
من نگویم چه کن ار اهل دلی خود تو بگوی
I say not, do what. Of the men of heart (Sufis)[2] thou art Do thou thy self say.

سفله طبع است جهان بر کرمش تکیه مکن
Mean of nature, is the world on its generosity, rely not
ای جهان دیده ثبات قدم از سفله مجوی
O world-experienced one from the mean, stability of foot do not thou-seek.

March 26 - ۶ فروردین

خوشتر ز عیش و صحبت و باغ و بهار چیست
More pleasant than the pleasure (the manifestations of glories of the Absolute One, God) and the enjoyment of the garden and the spring (the world, adorned with trees and flowers) is what?
ساقی کجاست گو سبب انتظار چیست
Where is the Saki (the Murshid) Say: "The cause of our waiting is what?

هر وقت خوش که دست دهد مغتنم شمار
Every pleasant moment that appeareth, reckon plunder;
کس را وقوف نیست که انجام کار چیست
Delay is to none. For the end of work is what?

1- Tapster
2- A Muslim ascetic and mystic

۷ فروردین - March 27

دوش می‌آمد و رخساره برافروخته بود
Last night, He (the true Beloved) came and His cheek, He had enkindled.

تا کجا باز دل غمزده‌ای سوخته بود
Let us see, the grief-stricken heart (of the lover) how He had consumed

رسم عاشق کشی و شیوه شهرآشوبی
The custom of lover-slaying and the way of city-up setting

جامه‌ای بود که بر قامت او دوخته بود
Was a garment that, on His form, He had stitched

۸ فروردین - March 28

شب صحبت غنیمت دان که بعد از روزگار ما
The night of society, (with beloved ones) reckon plunder. For, after our time

بسی گردش کند گردون بسی لیل و نهار آرد
The sphere many a revolution maketh; many a night (winter) and day (spring) bringeth.

بهار عمر خواه ای دل وگرنه این چمن هر سال
O heart! desire the spring season. If not, every year, this sward (the world)

چو نسرین صد گل آرد بار و چون بلبل هزار آرد
A hundred beautiful roses. like the wild rose, and a thousand (birds) like the nightingale bringeth.

۹ فروردین - March 29

مباش در پی آزار و هر چه خواهی کن
Be not in the pursuit of injury: do whatever (else) thou desirest:

که در شریعت ما غیر از این گناهی نیست
For in our Shariat, save this, a sin is none.

عنان کشیده رو ای پادشاه کشور حسن
O King of the dominion of beauty! go rein (impetuously) drawn:

که نیست بر سر راهی که دادخواهی نیست
For at the head of a street, is it not a justice-seeker is none?

۱۰ فروردین - March 30

هرگز نمیرد آن که دلش زنده شد به عشق
Never dieth that one, whose heart is alive with (true) love(to God):

ثبت است بر جریده عالم دوام ما
On the world's record, is written the everlasting existence of ours.

چندان بود کرشمه و ناز سهی قدان
The coy glance and the grace of those straight of stature (illusory beloved ones) (is only) till

کاید به جلوه سرو صنوبرخرام ما
With grace, moving like a lofty pine-tree, cometh the cypress of (the true Beloved) ours.

۱۱ فروردین - March 31

ابرآذاری بر آمد باد نوروزی وزید
Come up hath the cloud azar[1] (and) blown hath the breeze of nau-ruz

وجه می میخواهم و مطرب که میگوید رسید
The way of wine, I desire and the minstrel who singeth hath arrived

شاهدان در جلوه و من شرمسار کیسهام
In splendour (of beauty) the lovely (beloved) ones (are and), ashamed of my empty purse, I am

بار عشق و مفلسی صعب است میباید کشید
O sky! This shamefulness, how long shall I endure?

۱۲ فروردین - April 1

مجلس انس و بهار و بحث شعر اندر میان
In the midst, the assembly of friends, and spring, and the discourse of love

نستدن جام می از جانان گران جانی بود
Not to take the cup of wine from the beloved, slow-souledness is.

دی عزیزی گفت حافظ میخورد پنهان شراب
Last night, a dear one (a follower of the shara') said Secretly, Hafiz drinketh wine.

ای عزیز من نه عیب آن به که پنهانی بود
O dear one the sin best that, which a secret is

1-The sixth month is the Roman month

۱۳ فروردین - April 2

صبا به تهنیت پیر می فروش آمد
For the congratulation of the Pir[1], wine-seller, (Muhammad) the morning-breeze (Jibrail) came
که موسم طرب و عیش و ناز و نوش آمد
Saying: "The season of joy, and of pleasure, and of freshness, and of sweet ness is came.

تنور لاله چنان برفروخت باد بهار
The oven (of beauty and of splendour) of the tulip the spring-breeze enkindled to such a degree, '
که غنچه غرق عرق گشت و گل به جوش آمد
That, immersed in sweat (of the rose – water) bud became; and into agitation, the rose came.

۱۴ فروردین - April 3

آسمان بار امانت نتوانست کشید
The load of deposit (of love and of divine knowledge), the (lofty) sky could not endure:
قرعه کار به نام من دیوانه زدند
In the name of helpless me, the dice of the work, (of deposit of love) they cast.

جنگ هفتاد و دو ملت همه را عذر بنه
The wrangle of seventy-two sects, establish excuse for all
چون ندیدند حقیقت ره افسانه زدند
When truth, they saw not, the door of feeble they beat.

۱۵ فروردین - April 4

بهار و گل طرب انگیز گشت و توبه شکن
Joy-exciting and repentance-shattering became the spring and the rose
به شادی رخ گل، بیخ غم ز دل برکن
With the joy of the face of the rose, grief's root from the heart up-pluck.

رسید باد صبا غنچه در هواداری
Arrived the morning-breeze from passion-possessing (love) the rose-bud,
ز خود برون شد و بر خود درید پیراهن
Out from itself, went and on itself the shirt rent (blossomed)

1-A Muslim saint or holy man, Pietist

۱۶ فروردین - April 5

چو غنچه گر چه فروبستگیست کار جهان
Though like the (closed up) rose-bud, the world's work is a closed up knot,
تو همچو باد بهاری گره گشا می‌باش
Like the spring-breeze, thou, the knot (bud) opener be.
وفا مجوی ز کس ور سخن نمی‌شنوی
From none, seek fidelity and if, my speech, thou hear not,
به هرزه طالب سیمرغ و کیمیا می‌باش
In foolishness, seeker of the simurg hand of alchemy be.

۱۷ فروردین - April 6

چه جورها که کشیدند بلبلان از دی
From December, what tyrannies (they were) that the bulbuls[1] endured
به بوی آن که دگر نوبهار بازآید
In the hope that, again, the fresh spring may come back.
ز نقش بند قضا هست امید آن حافظ
Hafiz from the painter of destiny (God) hope of that is
که همچو سرو به دستم نگار بازآید
That, to my hand, like the cypress, the idol may come back

۱۸ فروردین - April 7

با خراباتیان نشینان ز کرامات ملاف
With the tavern-haunters, boast not of generosity:
هر سخن وقتی و هر نکته مکانی دارد
Every word, a time; every subtlety, a place hath.
مرغ زیرک نزند در چمنش پرده سرای
The wise bird (the lover, sincere in love's claim) goeth not, song-singing, in its sward of beauty,
هر بهاری که به دنباله خزانی دارد
Every spring (beloved) in whose rear, an autumn (of effacement) hath.

1-Nightingale

۱۹ فروردین - April 8

به عزم توبه سحر گفتم استخاره کنم
In the morning, with the desire of repentance, (to my heart) I said: "I seek the counsel of God,"
بهار توبه شکن می‌رسد چه چاره کنم
Spring, repentance-shatterer, ariveth what remedy may I make

سخن درست بگویم نمی‌توانم دید
True speech, I utter: I cannot see (that this state is very difficult)
که می خورند حریفان و من نظاره کنم
For the companions drink wine and looking on I make.

۲۰ فروردین - April 9

در تنگنای حیرتم از نخوت رقیب
From the watcher's pomp, I am in the strait of astonishment
یا رب مباد آن که گدا معتبر شود
O Lord! forbid that revered, the beggar should be.

بس نکته غیر حسن بباید که تا کسی
Besides beauty, many a subtlety is necessary, so that a person
مقبول طبع مردم صاحب نظر شود
Acceptable to the disposition of one possessed of vision, should be

۲۱ فروردین - April 10

بتی دارم که گرد گل ز سنبل سایه بان دارد
I have an idol that, the canopy of the hyacinth around the rose hath:
بهار عارضش خطی به خون ارغوان دارد
A line in the blood of the Arghavan[1], the spring of his cheek hath

چو عاشق می‌شدم گفتم که بردم گوهر مقصود
When I became lover,(of God) I spake saying: "I have carried off the jewel of my desire (union with God)
ندانستم که این دریا چه موج خون فشان دارد
I knew not what (tumultuous), blood-scattering, waves, this sea (of unity) hath

---

1-Flower

April 11 - ۲۲ فروردین

رسم بدعهدی ایام چو دید ابر بهار
When, the spring-cloud beheld Time's bad faith,
گریه‌اش بر سمن و سنبل و نسرین آمد
On the lily and the hyacinth and the rose, its weeping came.
چون صبا گفته حافظ بشنید از بلبل
When, from the nightingale, the morning breeze heard Hafez's utterance,
عنبرافشان به تماشای ریاحین آمد
At the spectacle of the sweet basil, ambergris scattering, it (the breeze) came.

April 12 - ۲۳ فروردین

مکن ز غصه شکایت که در طریق طلب
Complain not of grief. For in the path of search,
به راحتی نرسید آن که زحمتی نکشید
That one who endured not trouble (even) to a little ease, arrived not
بهار می‌گذرد دادگسترا دریاب
The spring passeth. O justice-dispenser help
که رفت موسم و حافظ هنوز می‌نچشید
For, departed hath the sea son and not yet hath Hafiz tasted wine

April 13 - ۲۴ فروردین

صوفی گلی بچین و مرقع به خار بخش
Sufi[1] a beautiful rose pluck and to the thorn the patched religious garment, give
وین زهد خشک را به می خوشگوار بخش
For pleasant tasting wine, this thy dry austerity, give
زهد گران که شاهد و ساقی نمی‌خرند
Excessive austerity that the lovely one and the Zahid[2] purchase not
در حلقه چمن به نسیم بهار بخش
In the sward's ring (time) to spring's fragrant breeze, give.

1-A Muslim ascetic and mystic
2-Pietist

۲۵ فروردین - April 14

رقصیدن سرو و حالت گل
The dancing of the cypress, and the rapture of the rose,
بی صوت هزار خوش نباشد
Without the one thousand songs is not pleasant.

با یار شکرلب گل اندام
With the beloved, sugar of lip, rose of body,
بی بوس و کنار خوش نباشد
(To be) Without kiss and embrace is not pleasant.

۲۶ فروردین - April 15

ساق بهار می‌رسد و وجه می‌نماند
Saki[1] spring arriveth and means of wine (drinking) is none
فکری بکن که خون دل آمد ز غم به جوش
(On getting means) a thought make. For, from grief (of want of means of wine – drinking) into tumult hath come my heart's blood.

عشق است و مفلسی و جوانی و نوبهار
Love and poverty, and youth, and the new spring, (all this) is
عذرم پذیر و جرم به ذیل کرم بپوش
My excuse. It, accept and, in mercy's trail, the crime conceal.

۲۷ فروردین - April 16

گر بهار عمر باشد باز بر تخت چمن
If on the sward's throne, again be the spring of life,
چتر گل در سر کشی ای مرغ خوشخوان غم مخور
O bird, night-singing over thy head, thou mayst draw the canopy of the rose suffer not grief

دور گردون گر دو روزی بر مراد ما نرفت
If, for a space of two days, to our desire, the sphere's revolutions turned not
دایما یکسان نباشد حال دوران غم مخور
Ever, in one way, the state of revolution is not suffer not grief.

1-Tapster

April 17 - ۲۸ فروردین

در اندرون من خسته دل ندانم کیست
Within this shattered heart, I know not who is.
که من خموشم و او در فغان و در غوغاست
For, I am silent; and in clamour and tumult, it (my heart, in which is the true Beloved) is.
دلم ز پرده برون شد کجایی ای مطرب
Forth from the screen, went my heart. O Minstrel! where art thou?
بنال هان که از این پرده کار ما به نواست
Ho! sing. For, on account of this note, in melody, our work is.

April 18 - ۲۹ فروردین

سخن در پرده می‌گویم چو گل از غنچه بیرون آی
Within the screen, speech I utter forth from (thyself), like the rose-bud (from the bud) come
که بیش از پنج روزی نیست حکم میر نوروزی
For, not more than a space of five days, is the order of the chief of a nau-ruz
ندانم نوحه قمری به طرف جویباران چیست
The lament of the turtle-dove by the marge of the stream, I know not where-fore it is
مگر او نیز همچون من غمی دارد شبانروزی
Perchance, like me, a grief it hath night and day

April 19 - ۳۰ فروردین

من ملک بودم و فردوس برین جایم بود
The angel, I was and loftiest paradise was my abode
آدم آورد در این دیر خراب آبادم
Into this ruined cloister (this world) me, Adam brought,
سایه طوبی و دلجویی حور و لب حوض
The shade of the Tuba tree, and the heart-seekingness of the Hur[1], and the marge of the pool (Kausar)
به هوای سر کوی تو برفت از یادم
(All) In desire of the head of Thy street, passed from my mind.

1-Lover

۳۱ فروردین - April 20

مژده ای دل که دگر باد صبا بازآمد
O heart! glad tidings that the morning breeze hath come back,
هدهد خوش خبر از طرف سبا بازآمد
From the quarters of Saba (the land of Queen Balkis) the lapwing of good news hath come back.

برکش ای مرغ سحر نغمه داوودی باز
O bird of the morning! (the bulbul, or the dove) Prolong the melody of Dawood:
که سلیمان گل از باد هوا بازآمد
For from the quarter of the air, the So leiman of the rose hath come back.

فصل بهار
(Spring)
اردیبهشت
May

۱ اردیبهشت - April 21

میر من خوش میروی کاندر سر و پا میرمت

My Lord! sweetly, Thou goest in so much that in Thee, head to foot (altogether) I die

خوش خرامان شو که پیش قد رعنا میرمت

My Bold One sweetly, Thou movest before Thee, I die.

گفته بودی کی بمیری پیش من تعجیل چیست

Thou saidest Before me, when wilt thou die Why is haste

خوش تقاضا می کنی پیش تقاضا میرمت

A sweet demand, Thou makest. (Even) before Thy demand I die.

۲ اردیبهشت - April 22

عاشقی را که چنین باده شبگیر دهند

That Aref[1] (lover), to whom they give wine like this, night-watching

کافر عشق بود گر نشود باده پرست

Is infidel to love, if he be not wine-worshipper.

برو ای زاهد و بر دردکشان خرده مگیر

O Zahed! go seize not a small matter against the drinkers of wine-dregs

که ندادند جز این تحفه به ما روز الست

For, save this gift (of dregs), naught did they give us on the day of Alast.

۳ اردیبهشت - April 23

صنما با غم عشق تو چه تدبیر کنم

O idol with grief of love for thee what plaint, shall I make?

تا به کی در غم تو ناله شبگیر کنم

In grief for thee, till when the night-seizing wail shall I make?

دل دیوانه از آن شد که نصیحت شنود

Passed (to the true Beloved) my distraught heart on that account that a Remedy It Might accept

مگرش هم ز سر زلف تو زنجیر کنم

Perchance, with Thy tress-tip, its chain I may make.

1-Mystic

۴ اردیبهشت - April 24

ای خرم از فروغ رخت لاله زار عمر
O thou, from the splendour of whose cheek, is joyous the tulip-bed of life
بازآ که ریخت بی گل رویت بهار عمر
Come back for, without the rose of thy cheek, spilleth the spring of life.

از دیده گر سرشک چو باران چکد رواست
If, like rain, the tear drop from my eye, it is lawful
کاندر غمت چو برق بشد روزگار عمر
For, in grief for thee, like lightning (swiftly in tumult) passed the time of life.

۵ اردیبهشت - April 25

به صوت بلبل و قمری اگر ننوشی می
If to the voice of the bulbul[1] and of the turtle-dove, wine thou drink not;
علاج کی کنمت آخرالدواء الکی
Thee, how may I cure The last remedy is the cautery.

ذخیره‌ای بنه از رنگ و بوی فصل بهار
Of the colour and perfume of the spring season, lay up
که می‌رسند ز پی رهزنان بهمن و دی
For keep arriving in pursuit the highway men, autumn and winter

۶ اردیبهشت - April 26

آدمی در عالم خاکی نمی‌آید به دست
In this dusty world, to hand cometh not a man
عالمی دیگر بباید ساخت و از نو آدمی
It is necessary to make another world, and a new a man.

خیز تا خاطر بدان ترک سمرقندی دهیم
Arise. To the saucy ones of Samarkand, let us give our heart
کز نسیمش بوی جوی مولیان آید همی
For, from its breeze, the fragrance of the river Mulian (the Oxus) cometh anon.

1-Nightingale

April 27 - ۷ اردیبهشت

پیر دردی کش ما گر چه ندارد زر و زور
Although neither gold, nor force, hath our Pir, dreg-drinking,
خوش عطابخش و خطاپوش خدایی دارد
Happily, a God sin-forgiving, error-covering, he hath.

محترم دار دلم کاین مگس قندپرست
(O true Beloved) Keep my heart great. For this sugar-worshipping fly, (the heart)
تا هواخواه تو شد فر همایی دارد
Since Thy desire it became, the pomp of the (auspicious) Homa hath.

April 28 - ۸ اردیبهشت

هواخواه توام جانا و می‌دانم که می‌دانی
O true Beloved Thy well-wisher, I am, and (this) I know that Thou knowest
که هم نادیده می‌بینی و هم ننوشته می‌خوانی
For, both the un-seen, Thou seest; and also the un-written (by fate) Thou readest.

ملامتگو چه دریابد میان عاشق و معشوق
Of the mystery of the lover and of the Beloved, what gaineth the reproacher
نبیند چشم نابینا خصوص اسرار پنهانی
The non-seeing eye especially seeth not a secret mystery.

April 29 - ۹ اردیبهشت

ما را که درد عشق و بلای خمار کشت
Since love's pain is ours, and the calamity of wine-sickness,
یا وصل دوست یا می صافی دوا کند
(Its remedy) either the ruby (lip) of the beloved, or the pure wine maketh.

جان رفت در سر می و حافظ به عشق سوخت
In the desire of wine, life passed; and in love Hafez consumed:
عیسی دمی کجاست که احیای ما کند
Where is one of Isa-breath (life-giving) that our reviving maketh

April 30 - ۱۰ اردیبهشت

زلف آشفته و خوی کرده و خندان لب و مست
(The Beloved) Tress dishevelled; sweat expressed; lip laughing; intoxicated.

پیرهن چاک و غزل خوان و صراحی در دست
Garment rent; song-singing; goblet in His hand;

نرگسش عربده جوی و لبش افسوس کنان
Eye, contest-seeking; lip lamenting

نیم شب دوش به بالین من آمد بنشست
Came, at midnight, last night, to my pillow; (and there); sate.

May 1 - ۱۱ اردیبهشت

بارها گفته‌ام و بار دگر می‌گویم
Times I have said and again I say,

که من دلشده این ره نه به خود می‌پویم
That, heart bereft, not of myself, have I gone this Path (of love)

در پس آینه طوطی صفتم داشته‌اند
Behind the (pure) mirror me, (of the holy traveller's heart) they have kept like the parrot

آن چه استاد ازل گفت بگو می‌گویم
What the Teacher of eternity without beginning said Say I say.

May 2 - ۱۲ اردیبهشت

مرحبا ای پیک مشتاقان بده پیغام دوست
Welcome! O Messenger of the Longing Ones give the message of the Friend.

تا کنم جان از سر رغبت فدای نام دوست
That, with the essence of pleasure, I may make my soul a sacrifice for the Friend.

واله و شیداست دایم همچو بلبل در قفس
Wailing and lamenting perpetually is like the nightingale in the cage:

طوطی طبعم ز عشق شکر و بادام دوست
Of parrot-nature am I through love of sugar (the lip) and of the almond (the eye) of the Friend.

۱۳ اردیبهشت - May 3

ما ز یاران چشم یاری داشتیم
The eye (of expectation) of friendship from friends we had
خود غلط بود آن چه ما پنداشتیم
Verily, 'twas mistake that which we thought

تا درخت دوستی برگی دهد
Let us see, when fruit, the tree of friend ship will give
حالیا رفتیم و تخمی کاشتیم
Now, we have departed and a seed (zikr va fikr) we have sown.

۱۴ اردیبهشت - May 4

برخاست بوی گل ز در آشتی درآی
(O beloved) Hath risen the perfume, of the rose by the door of friend ship come (and union choose)
ای نوبهار ما رخ فرخنده فال تو
O fresh spring of ours the auspicious face (is) the omen of Thine.

تا آسمان ز حلقه به گوشان ما شود
So that (of the crowd) of our beringed ones (slaves) the sky may be,
کو عشوه‌ای ز ابروی همچون هلال تو
Where, the charm of an eye-brow like the new (crescent) moon of Thine

۱۵ اردیبهشت - May 5

گفتم ای سلطان خوبان رحم کن بر این غریب
(To the true Beloved) I said: "O Sultan of lovely ones! show pity to this poor stranger."
گفت در دنبال دل ره گم کند مسکین غریب
He said: "In the desire of his own heart, loseth his way the wretched stranger."

گفتمش مگذر زمانی گفت معذورم بدار
To Him, I said: "Pass awhile with me." He replied: "Hold me excused."
خانه پروردی چه تاب آرد غم چندین غریب
A home (delicately) nurtured one, what care beareth he for such griefs of the poor stranger?

۱۶ اردیبهشت - May 6

سینه از آتش دل در غم جانانه بسوخت
From the fire (of love) of my heart, my chest in grief for the Beloved consumed.
آتشی بود در این خانه که کاشانه بسوخت
In this house, (of the heart), was (such) a fire, that the house consumed.
تنم از واسطه دوری دلبر بگداخت
From the farness of the Heart-Ravisher, my body melted (waned):
جانم از آتش مهر رخ جانانه بسوخت
From Love's fire for the Beloved's face, my soul consumed.

۱۷ اردیبهشت - May 7

خلوت گزیده را به تماشا چه حاجت است
To him that hath chosen solitude, of the spectacle is what need?
چون کوی دوست هست به صحرا چه حاجت است
When the street of the Beloved is, (at hand) of the desert is what need?
جانا به حاجتی که تو را هست با خدا
O Soul! By the need of God that is thine,
کاخر دمی بپرس که ما را چه حاجت است
At last, a moment, ask, saying: "Ours is what need?"

۱۸ اردیبهشت - May 8

میان گریه می‌خندم که چون شمع اندر این مجلس
In the midst of weeping, I laugh. Because, like the candle in this assembly,
زبان آتشینم هست لیکن در نمی‌گیرد
The fiery tongue is mine; but (it, the tongue) it (the fire) kindleth not.
چه خوش صید دلم کردی بنازم چشم مستت را
How happily Thou madest prey of my heart! Of Thy intoxicated eye, I boast:
که کس مرغان وحشی را از این خوشتر نمی‌گیرد
For, better than this, the wild birds, a person taketh not.

۱۹ اردیبهشت - May 9

کس نیست که افتاده آن زلف دوتا نیست
Who is not fallen into that doubled tress is none;
در رهگذر کیست که دامی ز بلا نیست
In whose path is it, that a snare of calamity is none

چون چشم تو دل می‌برد از گوشه نشینان
Since from the corner-sitters Thy eye ravished my heart:
همراه تو بودن گنه از جانب ما نیست
To be thy train, a sin on our part is none.

۲۰ اردیبهشت - May 10

ای غایب از نظر به خدا می‌سپارمت
O (beloved) hidden from sight! to God, I entrust, thee.
جانم بسوختی و به دل دوست دارمت
(In pain of separation) Thou consumedest my soul; yet with heart, friend I hold thee.

تا دامن کفن نکشم زیر پای خاک
So long as I trail not the skirt of my shroud beneath the foot of the dust, (of the grave),
باور مکن که دست ز دامن بدارمت
Believe not, I will keep(my)hand from off the skirt of thee.

۲۱ اردیبهشت - May 11

به یاد چشم تو خود را خراب خواهم ساخت
In memory of Thy eye, myself ruined I will make:
بنای عهد قدیم استوار خواهم کرد
The foundation of the ancient covenant, strong I will make.

صبا کجاست که این جان خون گرفته چو گل
Where is the breeze? (the angel of death) For this life, blood gathered, like the (ruddy, opening) rose,
فدای نکهت گیسوی یار خواهم کرد
A sacrifice for the perfume of the (true) Beloved's tress, I will make.

May 12 - ۲۲ اردیبهشت

میان عاشق و معشوق فرق بسیار است
Between the lover and the beloved, great is the difference
چو یار ناز نماید شما نیاز کنید
(O lovers) When the beloved showeth disdain, supplication make ye

نخست موعظه پیر صحبت این حرف است
The first counsel of the Pir (Murshid) of the assembly was this world
که از مصاحب ناجنس احتراز کنید
From ignoble associates shunning make ye.

May 13 - ۲۳ اردیبهشت

گر نور عشق حق به دل و جانت اوفتد
When, on thy heart and soul, the light of God's love falleth,
بالله کز آفتاب فلک خوبتر شوی
By God (I swear) that fairer than the sky's resplendent sun thou shalt be

یک دم غریق بحر خدا شو گمان مبر
A moment, immersed in God's sea, be; think not,
کز آب هفت بحر به یک موی تر شوی
That, to the extent of a single hair, with the water of seven (all the) seas (of the world) wet, thou shalt be.

May 14 - ۲۴ اردیبهشت

خرم آن روز کز این منزل ویران بروم
Joyous that day when from this desolate abode I go
راحت جان طلبم و از پی جانان بروم
The ease of soul (the true Beloved) I seek and for the sake of the Beloved I go.

گر چه دانم که به جایی نبرد راه غریب
Though I know that to such a place the stranger findeth not the path
من به بوی سر آن زلف پریشان بروم
To the sweet perfume of that dishevelled tress, I go.

May 15 - ۲۵ اردیبهشت

گل در بر و می در کف و معشوق به کام است
(When) The rose is in the bosom; wine in the hand; and the Beloved to my desire,
سلطان جهانم به چنین روز غلام است
On such a day, the world's Sultan is my slave.

گو شمع میارید در این جمع که امشب
Say: Into this assembly, bring ye no candle for to-night.
در مجلس ما ماه رخ دوست تمام است
In our assembly, the moon of the Friend's face is full.

May 16 - ۲۶ اردیبهشت

گر پیر مغان مرشد من شد چه تفاوت
If the Pir of the Magians become my Murshid what difference?
در هیچ سری نیست که سری ز خدا نیست
There is no head, in which a mystery of God is none.

عاشق چه کند گر نکشد بار ملامت
Against the sun resplendent to speak saying: I am the fountain of light.
با هیچ دلاور سپر تیر قضا نیست
Worthy even of obscure Suha, the great ones know is none.

May 17 - ۲۷ اردیبهشت

مرا عهدیست با جانان که تا جان در بدن دارم
With the true Beloved, a covenant is mine that As long as in body, life I have
هواداران کویش را چو جان خویشتن دارم
The well-wishers of His street, (dear) like my own (precious) life hold.

صفای خلوت خاطر از آن شمع چگل جویم
By that candle of Chigil (the true Beloved) the purity of the khilvat[1] of my heart, I be hold
فروغ چشم و نور دل از آن ماه ختن دارم
From that moon of Khutan[2], the splendour of my eye and the luminosity of heart, I have.

1-Solitude
2-Beautiful beloved

۲۸ اردیبهشت - May 18

بشنو این نکته که خود را ز غم آزاده کنی
This my subtlety, hear that, free from grief, thyself thou mayst make
خون خوری گر طلب روزی ننهاده کنی
Blood (of grief) thou drinkest, if search for victuals, not placed (intended for thee) in thou makest.

آخرالامر گل کوزه گران خواهی شد
In the end, the clay of the goglet-maker (potters) thou wilt become;
حالیا فکر سبو کن که پر از باده کنی
Now, think of the pitcher (of thy heart) that, it, full of wine (of ma'rifat and of love) thou mayst make

۲۹ اردیبهشت - May 19

خمی که ابروی شوخ تو در کمان انداخت
The great curve that, into the bow, (of thy eye-brow), thy told eye-brow cast,
به قصد جان من زار ناتوان انداخت
In design of the blood of me, miserable, powerless, it cast.

نبود نقش دو عالم که رنگ الفت بود
Not the picture (of existence) of the two worlds was, when was the color of love:
زمانه طرح محبت نه این زمان انداخت
Not at this time, Love's foundation, did Time cast.

۳۰ اردیبهشت - May 20

هر آن که جانب اهل خدا نگه دارد
(O true Beloved) Everyone, who regardeth the people of fidelity (lovers of God)
خداش در همه حال از بلا نگه دارد
Him, in every state, from calamity God preserveth.

حدیث دوست نگویم مگر به حضرت دوست
Save in the Friend's presence, I utter not the tale of the Friend;
که آشنا سخن آشنا نگه دارد
For the speech of the friend, the friend preserveth.

May 21 - اردیبهشت ۳۱

دور فلکی یک سره بر منهج عدل است
(Now) Altogether, in the way of justice, is the sky's revolution
خوش باش که ظالم نبرد راه به منزل
Be happy that the tyrant taketh not the path to the stage (of his object)

حافظ قلم شاه جهان مقسم رزق است
Hafiz (when in) the (power of the) king of the world is the partition of subsistence,
از بهر معیشت مکن اندیشه باطل
For thy livelihood, make no useless thought

فصل بهار
(Spring)
خرداد
June

۱ خرداد - May 22

فکر بلبل همه آن است که گل شد یارش
The thought of the bulbul (the holy traveller) all is that, that the rose (the true Beloved) his beloved may be
گل در اندیشه که چون عشوه کند در کارش
The rose, in thought how, in her work, grace she may display.

دلربایی همه آن نیست که عاشق بکشند
Not all heart-ravishingness is that that slayeth the lover
خواجه آن است که باشد غم خدمتکارش
Khwaja is he, whose attendant is grief.

۲ خرداد - May 23

رفتم به باغ صبحدمی تا چنم گلی
One morning to the garden I went a rose to pluck
آمد به گوش ناگهم آواز بلبلی
Suddenly, came to my ear the clam our of a bulbul.

مسکین چو من به عشق گلی گشته مبتلا
Like me, wretched, in love for a rose, entangled he was
و اندر چمن فکنده ز فریاد غلغلی
And into the sward, by his plaint, cast a clamour.

۳ خرداد - May 24

چه مستیست ندانم که رو به ما آورد
I know not what is the intoxication that to us its face hath brought:
که بود ساقی و این باده از کجا آورد
Who is the cup-bearer? This wine, whence hath he brought?

تو نیز باده به چنگ آر و راه صحرا گیر
To thy hand, bring thou also the cup; take the path to the desert (and strive in pleasure);
که مرغ نغمه سرا ساز خوش نوا آورد
For, the sweet melody of song, the melody-warbling bird hath brought.

۴ خرداد - May 25

روزگاریست که سودای بتان دین من است
'Tis a (long) time since the passion for idols was my faith:
غم این کار نشاط دل غمگین من است
The pain of this work, the joy of the sorrowful heart of mine is.

دیدن روی تو را دیده جان بین باید
For beholding Thy ruby (lip), the soul-seeing eye is necessary:
وین کجا مرتبه چشم جهان بین من است
Where this rank for the world-seeing eye of mine is.

۵ خرداد - May 26

سر ارادت ما و آستان حضرت دوست
(Together are) The head of our desire, and the threshold of the Mighty Friend (God):
که هر چه بر سر ما می‌رود ارادت اوست
For, whatever (of good, or of bad) passeth over our head is His will.

نظیر دوست ندیدم اگر چه از مه و مهر
My Friend's equal, I have not seen; although (gleaming) of the moon and of the shining sun,
نهادم آینه‌ها در مقابل رخ دوست
The mirrors opposite to the Friend's face I placed.

۶ خرداد - May 27

ز گریه مردم چشمم نشسته در خون است
(O true Beloved) from (much), the pupil of my eye seated in blood (of grief) is,
ببین که در طلبت حال مردمان چون است
(From this) Behold the state of men in search of Thee, how it is.

به یاد لعل تو و چشم مست میگونت
To the memory of Thy ruby (lip) and wine-like (ruddy) intoxicated eye,
ز جام غم می لعلی که می‌خورم خون است
From griefs cup, the wine of that ruby that I drink, blood is.

May 28 - ۷ خرداد

راهیست راه عشق که هیچش کناره نیست
Love's path is Path whereof the shore is none:
آن جا جز آن که جان بسپارند چاره نیست
And there, unless they surrender their soul, remedy is none.

هر گه که دل به عشق دهی خوش دمی بود
Every moment that to love thou givest thy heart is a happy moment,
در کار خیر حاجت هیچ استخاره نیست
In the right work, need of praying to God to be directed aright is none.

May 29 - ۸ خرداد

منم که گوشه میخانه خانقاه من است
Such a one am I that the tavern-corner is the cloister of mine:
دعای پیر مغان ورد صبحگاه من است
The prayer from the Pir of Moghan is the morning task of mine.

گرم ترانه چنگ صبوح نیست چه باک
Although the melody of the harp of the morning be not mine, what fear?
نوای من به سحر آه عذرخواه من است
At morning-time (the resurrection) my cry is the excuse-utterer of mine.

May 30 - ۹ خرداد

گفتم صنم پرست مشو با صمد نشین
I said: "In the society of the lofty-sitter, be not idol worshipper?"
گفتا به کوی عشق هم این و هم آن کنند
He said: "In love's street, also this and also that (talk) they make"

گفتم هوای میکده غم می‌برد ز دل
I said: "The desire of the wine-house taketh grief from the heart."
گفتا خوش آن کسان که دلی شادمان کنند
He said: "Happy, those who joyous a single heart make."

May 31 - خرداد ۱۰

دیشب به سیل اشک ره خواب می‌زدم
Last night, with a torrent of tears, sleep's path, I dashed

نقشی به یاد خط تو بر آب می‌زدم
In memory of Thy down, a (vanishing) picture on water, I dashed.

ابروی یار در نظر و خرقه سوخته
In my view, the Friend's eye-brow; and the consumed Khirka

جامی به یاد گوشه محراب می‌زدم
To the memory of the corner of Thy prayer-arch (eye–brow) a cup I dashed.

June 1 - خرداد ۱۱

تو و طوبی و ما و قامت یار
(O Zahid) Thou and the Tuba tree; and we and the form of the (true) Beloved;

فکر هر کس به قدر همت اوست
Every one's thought (of arrangement of affairs) is to the limit of ambition of His.

گر من آلوده دامنم چه عجب
If I be soiled of skirt, what loss?

همه عالم گواه عصمت اوست
For the whole world is the evidence of the innocence of His.

June 2 - خرداد ۱۲

دارم امید عاطفتی از جانب دوست
Of a great favor from the threshold of the Friend (God), hope mine is.

کردم جنایتی و امیدم به عفو اوست
A great sin I have done; of His pardon hope mine, is.

دانم که بگذرد ز سر جرم من که او
I know that He will pass by (forgive) my sin; for

گر چه پریوش است ولیکن فرشته خوست
Although, Pari-like (vengeful and omnipotent) He is, of angel-nature (merciful and compassionate) He is,

June 3 - ۱۳ خرداد

دل دادمش به مژده و خجلت همی‌برم
For his glad tidings, I gave him my heart; and, I bear shame
زین نقد قلب خویش که کردم نثار دوست
Of this coin of little value wherewith I bescattered the Friend.

شکر خدا که از مدد بخت کارساز
Thanks to God that, by the aid of concordant Fortune,
بر حسب آرزوست همه کار و بار دوست
All my work is to the desire of the Friend

June 4 - ۱۴ خرداد

دل صنوبریم همچو بید لرزان است
My pine cone-like heart is trembling like the willow,
ز حسرت قد و بالای چون صنوبر دوست
In envy of the form and the pine-like stature of the Friend.

اگر چه دوست به چیزی نمی‌خرد ما را
Although, the Friend purchase us not for even a small thing,
به عالمی نفروشیم مویی از سر دوست
For a whole world, we sell not a single hair from the head of the Friend.

June 5 - ۱۵ خرداد

عاشق که شد که یار به حالش نظر نکرد
Lover, who became, at whose state the true Beloved gazed not?
ای خواجه درد نیست وگرنه طبیب هست
O Sir! (The truth is) there is no pain. Otherwise, the Physician (God) is.

فریاد حافظ این همه آخر به هرزه نیست
In short, all this lament of Hafez is not in vain:
هم قصه‌ای غریب و حدیثی عجیب هست
Both a strange story and a wonderful tale, it is

۱۶ خرداد - June 6

پیرانه سرم عشق جوانی به سر افتاد
Elderly of head, into my head youthful love, hath fallen:
وان راز که در دل بنهفتم به درافتاد
And that mystery (of love) that, in the heart, I concealed, out hath fallen.

از راه نظر مرغ دلم گشت هواگیر
From vision's path, the bird of my heart went soaring.
ای دیده نگه کن که به دام که درافتاد
O eye! (of my heart) behold into whose snare, it (the bird of the heart) hath fallen.

۱۷ خرداد - June 7

درد ما را نیست درمان الغیاث
For our pain, is no remedy, Justice
هجر ما را نیست پایان الغیاث
For our separation is no end, Justice

دین و دل بردند و قصد جان کنند
Religion and the heart, they ravish and make design upon our
الغیاث از جور خوبان الغیاث
Justice against the tyranny of lovely ones, Justice

۱۸ خرداد - June 8

یا رب آن شاهوش ماه رخ زهره جبین
O Lord! that one, king-like, moon of face, Venus of forehead,
در یکتای که و گوهر یک دانه کیست
The inestimable pearl of whom; and the incomparable jewel of whom is?

گفتم آه از دل دیوانه حافظ بی تو
(To the beloved) I said "Without thee, sigh from the distraught heart of Hafez: "
زیر لب خنده زنان گفت که دیوانه کیست
Under the lip, (covertly) laughing, she spake, saying: He distraught of whom is?"

June 9 - خرداد ۱۹

یا رب این شمع دل افروز ز کاشانه کیست

O Lord! that candle, (the beloved) night-illuminating, (by her resplendent beauty) from the house of whom is?

جان ما سوخت بپرسید که جانانه کیست

Our soul hath consumed. Ask ye, saying: "She, the beloved, of whom is?"

حالیا خانه برانداز دل و دین من است

Now, the up-setter of my heart and of my religion, she is:

تا در آغوش که می‌خسبد و همخانه کیست

Let us see: she the fellow-sleeper of whom is; the fellow-lodger of whom is:

June 10 - خرداد ۲۰

ماهم این هفته برون رفت و به چشمم سالیست

From the city, my moon (the beloved) went this week; to my eye (by reason of pain of separation) a year it is:

حال هجران تو چه دانی که چه مشکل حالیست

The state of separation what knowest thou how difficult the state is?

مردم دیده ز لطف رخ او در رخ او

From the grace of her cheek, in her cheek, the pupil of my eye

عکس خود دید گمان برد که مشکین خالیست

Beheld its own reflection; and imagined that (on the Beloved's cheek) a musky (dark) mole it is.

June 11 - خرداد ۲۱

عاقبت دست بدان سرو بلندش برسد

In the end, to that lofty cypress, reacheth the hand of him,

هر که را در طلبت همت او قاصر نیست

Whose spirit in search of Thee, defective is not.

از روان بخشی عیسی نزنم دم هرگز

Before Thee, I boast not of Isa's life-giving;

زان که در روح فزایی چو لبت ماهر نیست

For like Thy lip, in soul-refreshing, expert he ('Isa) is not.

June 12 - خرداد ۲۲

مردم دیده ما جز به رخت ناظر نیست
A gazer save upon Thy face, the pupil of our eye is not.
دل سرگشته ما غیر تو را ذاکر نیست
A remembrancer save of Thee, our overturned heart is not.

اشکم احرام طواف حرمت می‌بندد
My tear bindeth the Ihram of the Tawaf of Thy sacred enclosure.
گر چه از خون دل ریش دمی طاهر نیست
Although pure blood of the blood of my wounded heart, it (my tear) is not.

June 13 - خرداد ۲۳

هر چه هست از قامت ناساز بی اندام ماست
Whatever unfitness there is, is by reason of our unfit, formless form:
ور نه تشریف تو بر بالای کس کوتاه نیست
If not, on a person's stature, thy dress of honor, short is none.

بنده پیر خراباتم که لطفش دایم است
I am the slave of the Pir of the tavern, (the perfect Murshid) whose favor is constant:
ور نه لطف شیخ و زاهد گاه هست و گاه نیست
If not, the favor of the Shaikh and of the Zahed, is sometimes; and, sometimes is none.

June 14 - خرداد ۲۴

روشن از پرتو رویت نظری نیست که نیست
(O true Beloved) From the ray of Thy face, luminous a glance is not. that is not:
منت خاک درت بر بصری نیست که نیست
The favor of (collyrium) the dust of Thy door, on an eye is not, that is not.

ناظر روی تو صاحب نظرانند آری
Those possessed of sight (the prophets who, with the inward eye, behold the real beauty of God), are the spectator of Thy face. Yes:
سر گیسوی تو در هیچ سری نیست که نیست
The desire of Thy tress, in any, a desire is not, that is not.

June 15 - ۲۵ خرداد

عیب رندان مکن ای زاهد پاکیزه سرشت
O Zahed, pure of nature! censure not the profligates;
که گناه دگران بر تو نخواهند نوشت
For, against thee, they will not record another's crime.
من اگر نیکم و گر بد تو برو خود را باش
If I be good, (I am for myself) or if I be bad (I am for myself). Go thou: be thyself about thy work:
هر کسی آن درود عاقبت کار که کشت
In the end, everyone reapeth that work that he sowed.

June 16 - ۲۶ خرداد

ناامیدم مکن از سابقه لطف ازل
Of the former kindness (established) in eternity without beginning, make me not hopeless:
تو پس پرده چه دانی که که خوب است و که زشت
What knowest thou, behind the screen who is good, who is bad?
نه من از پرده تقوا به درافتادم و بس
From the cell of piety, not only I fell out:
پدرم نیز بهشت ابد از دست بهشت
My father (Adam) also let go from his hand Paradise of Eternity without end.

June 17 - ۲۷ خرداد

بلبلی برگ گلی خوش رنگ در منقار داشت
A nightingale had a rose-leaf, pleasant of hue in his beak
و اندر آن برگ و نوا خوش ناله‌های زار داشت
And, on that leaf and pleasant food, bitter lamentation held.
گفتمش در عین وصل این ناله و فریاد چیست
To him, I said: "In the very time of union (with the beloved) wherefore is this lament and cry?"
گفت ما را جلوه معشوق در این کار داشت
He said: "In this work (of lament), me the beloved's beauty held."

June 18 - ۲۸ خرداد

پنج روزی که در این مرحله مهلت داری
A space of five days (it is) that thou hast in this stage of favor;
خوش بیاسای زمانی که زمان این همه نیست
Rest pleasantly awhile. For Time all this is naught.

بر لب بحر فنا منتظریم ای ساقی
O Saki! We are waiting on the shore of the ocean of death
فرصتی دان که ز لب تا به دهان این همه نیست
Regard (it) again. For from lip to mouth all this is naught.

June 19 - ۲۹ خرداد

صبحدم مرغ چمن با گل نوخاسته گفت
At dawn, the bird of the sward (the necessarily existent One, God) spake to the rose (faithful men in the state of being beloved):
ناز کم کن که در این باغ بسی چون تو شکفت
"Display less disdain; for, in this garden (the world) many a one like thee hath blossomed."

گل بخندید که از راست نرنجیم ولی
The rose laughed saying: "We grieve not at the truth; but
هیچ عاشق سخن سخت به معشوق نگفت
No lover spoke a harsh word to the beloved."

June 20 - ۳۰ خرداد

سخن عشق نه آن است که آید به زبان
Not that which cometh to the tongue is the talk of love:
ساقیا می ده و کوتاه کن این گفت و شنفت
O Saki! (Murshid) give wine; make short this uttering and hearing.

اشک حافظ خرد و صبر به دریا انداخت
Into the sea, the tear of Hafez hath (so great is his weeping) cast wisdom and patience:
چه کند سوز غم عشق نیارست نهفت
What shall he do (Neither choice, nor power in his) The consuming of love's grief, he cannot conceal (and other remedy, he knoweth not).

June 21 - خرداد ۳۱

یا رب آن آهوی مشکین به ختن بازرسان
O lord that musky (fragrant) deer[1] (my beloved) back to Khutan[2] (safely) cause to reach

وان سهی سرو خرامان به چمن بازرسان
And back to the sward that straight, moving, cypress, cause to reach

دل آزرده ما را به نسیمی بنواز
With a breeze (of kindness) our withered fortune, cherish

یعنی آن جان ز تن رفته به تن بازرسان
That is that soul (the beloved) gone from the body, back to the body cause to reach

---

1-An allusion to the beloved
2-An allusion to the city of Shiraz

فصل تابستان (Summer)

تیر
July

۱ تیر - June 22

گل بی رخ یار خوش نباشد
Without the beloved's face, the rose is not pleasant.
بی باده بهار خوش نباشد
Without wine, spring is not pleasant.
طرف چمن و طواف بستان
The border of the sward and the air of the garden
بی لاله عذار خوش نباشد
Without the (beloved of) tulip cheek is not pleasant.

۲ تیر - June 23

بس که ما فاتحه و حرز یمانی خواندیم
Many the Fatiha and the Harz-i-Yamani[1] that we recited:
وز پی اش سوره اخلاص دمیدیم و برفت
After that, we murmured the wholeheartedness, and He departed.

عشوه دادند که بر ما گذری خواهی کرد
A glance, He gave saying: "From the street of desire (love), I depart not:"
دیدی آخر که چنین عشوه خریدیم و برفت
Thou sawest how, at last, we purchased the glance, and He departed.

۳ تیر - June 24

یا رب سببی ساز که یارم به سلامت
O Lord! devise a means, whereby in safety my Beloved
بازآید و برهاندم از بند ملامت
May come back and release me from the claw of reproach.
خاک ره آن یار سفرکرده بیارید
Bring ye the dust of the Path of that traveled Beloved (the necessarily existent One)
تا چشم جهان بین کنمش جای اقامت
That I may make my world-seeing eye His sojourn-place.

1- An effective and quickly answered prayer

June 25 - ۴ تیر

حسنت به اتفاق ملاحت جهان گرفت
By concord with darkish beauty, the world Thy beauty took.
آری به اتفاق جهان می‌توان گرفت
Yes; by concord, the world one can take.

افشای راز خلوتیان خواست کرد شمع
The revealing of the mysteries of the Khilvatis, the candle wished to make:
شکر خدا که سر دلش در زبان گرفت
Thanks to God! that its tongue (the candle's wick), the heart's desire kindled.

June 26 - ۵ تیر

از پای فتادیم چو آمد غم هجران
From our feet, we fell when separation's grief came:
در درد بمردیم چو از دست دوا رفت
In grief we remained when from the hand, the remedy passed.

دل گفت وصالش به دعا باز توان یافت
The heart said: "With prayer, one can again obtain (union with Him) passed."
عمریست که عمرم همه در کار دعا رفت
Tis a life-time since my life all in the work of prayer passed.

June 27 - ۶ تیر

شربتی از لب لعلش نچشیدیم و برفت
From His lip of ruby, a (single) draft we tasted not; and He departed:
روی مه پیکر او سیر ندیدیم و برفت
His face, moon of form, we beheld not to our fill; and He departed.

گویی از صحبت ما نیک به تنگ آمده بود
Thou mayst say: "By our society, He hath become greatly straitened."
بار بربست و به گردش نرسیدیم و برفت
His chattels, (thus quickly) He bound up: about him, we arrived not, and He departed.

June 28 - تیر ۷

شنیدهام سخنی خوش که پیر کنعان گفت
I heard a pleasant speech that the old man of Kan'an[1] (the Murshid) uttered:

فراق یار نه آن میکند که بتوان گفت
Separation from (want of acquisition of divine knowledge of) the true Beloved (God) maketh not that which can be uttered."

حدیث هول قیامت که گفت واعظ شهر
The tale of terror of the resurrection day, which the city-admonisher uttered?

کنایتیست که از روزگار هجران گفت
Is (only) a hint, which, of the time of separation, he uttered

June 29 - تیر ۸

در راه عشق مرحله قرب و بعد نیست
In love's Path, is no stage of nearness or of farness:

میبینمت عیان و دعا میفرستمت
(Hence, true Beloved) I clearly see Thee; and prayer, I send Thee.

هر صبح و شام قافلهای از دعای خیر
Every morning and evening, the Kafila of prayer for Thy welfare,

در صحبت شمال و صبا میفرستمت
In company with the (Cool) north and the east wind, I send Thee

June 30 - تیر ۹

دی پیر می فروش که ذکرش به خیر باد
Yesterday, the Pir[2], the wine-seller whose mention be for good!

گفتا شراب نوش و غم دل ببر ز یاد
Said: "Drink wine; and, from recollection, take the heart's grief."

گفتم به باد میدهدم باده نام و ننگ
I said: "To the wind, wine giveth my name and fame: "

گفتا قبول کن سخن و هر چه باد باد
He said: "Accept the word: be whatever be."

1- Ancient regions in southern Syria
2- A Muslim saint or holy man, Pietist

July 1 - تیر ۱۰

گفته لعل لبم هم درد بخشد هم دوا
Thou hast said My ruby lip giveth pain and also the remedy
گاه پیش درد و گه پیش مداوا میرمت
Sometimes before the pain and sometimes before the remedy, I die.

خوش خرامان می‌روی چشم بد از روی تو دور
Sweetly moving, Thou goest. Far, the evil eye from Thy face
دارم اندر سر خیال آن که در پا میرمت
In my head, I have a fancy that, at Thy feet, I die.

July 2 - تیر ۱۱

بیا که قصر امل سخت سست بنیادست
Come! For most unstable is the foundation of the Palace of Hope (the body, relying for permanency on external worship):
بیار باده که بنیاد عمر بر بادست
Bring the cup (of God's love); for the foundation of Life (of the soul) is (swiftly departing) on the (swift) wind.

غلام همت آنم که زیر چرخ کبود
Beneath the azure vault, I am that slave of resolution, who
ز هر چه رنگ تعلق پذیرد آزادست
Is free from whatever taketh color of attachment.

July 3 - تیر ۱۲

مدامم مست می‌دارد نسیم جعد گیسویت
Ever intoxicated keepeth me the waft of air of the tress-curl of Thine.
خرابم می‌کند هر دم فریب چشم جادویت
Momently ruined maketh me the deceit of the eye of sorcery of Thine.

پس از چندین شکیبایی شبی یا رب توان دیدن
O Lord! after such patience, one can see a night
که شمع دیده افروزیم در محراب ابرویت
Whereon, we may kindle the candle of our eye in the prayer-arch of the eyebrow of Thine

۱۳ تیر - July 4

نصیحتی کنمت یاد گیر و در عمل آر
Counsel, I proffer thee: take it to mind: bring it into action:
که این حدیث ز پیر طریقتم یادست
For, from the Pir of Tarikat[1] (the path), I recollect this matter.

غم جهان مخور و پند من مبر از یاد
Suffer not grief for the World: take not my counsel from thy mind:
که این لطیفه عشقم ز ره روی یادست
For, from a wayfarer, I recollect this sweet saying

۱۴ تیر - July 5

محراب ابرویت بنما تا سحرگهی
Display the prayer-arch of thy eye-brow, that, in the morning-time,
دست دعا برآرم و در گردن آرمت
(In excuse) I may bring forth my hand of prayer and bring it upon the neck of thee.

گر بایدم شدن سوی هاروت بابلی
If it be necessary for me to go to Harut of Babil,
صد گونه جادویی بکنم تا بیارمت
A hundred kinds of sorcery (learned from him) I will evoke to bring thee.

۱۵ تیر - July 6

ترسم که اشک در غم ما پرده در شود
I fear lest in respect of our grief the screen render should be
وین راز سر به مهر به عالم سمر شود
And in the world this sealed mystery a (revealed) tale should be

گویند سنگ لعل شود در مقام صبر
They say the stone becometh, in the stage of patience, the (precious) ruby
آری شود ولیک به خون جگر شود
Yes it becometh But (immersed) in blood, the liver should be

1-Principle, Sufism, religious way

۱۶ تیر - July 7

رندان تشنه لب را آبی نمی‌دهد کس
To profligates, thirsty of lip, none giveth (even) a little water:
گویی ولی شناسان رفتند از این ولایت
Thou mayest say: "Those recognizing holy men have departed from this land."

در زلف چون کمندش ای دل مپیچ کان جا
O heart! In His tress-like noose, twist not (and from its fancy come out); For, there,
سرها بریده بینی بی جرم و بی جنایت
Thou seest severed heads, crimeless, guiltless.

۱۷ تیر - July 8

هر آن کو خاطر مجموع و یار نازنین دارد
Everyone, who, his heart collected and the beloved acceptable hath,
سعادت همدم او گشت و دولت همنشین دارد
Happiness became his fellow-companion; and fortune, his fellow-sitter, he hath.

حریم عشق را درگه بسی بالاتر از عقل است
Much more lofty than reason is the court of the fold of love:
کسی آن آستان بوسد که جان در آستین دارد
That threshold, that one kisseth who, his life in his sleeve, hath.

۱۸ تیر - July 9

دل و دینم شد و دلبر به ملامت برخاست
Went heart and faith; and the Heart-Ravisher with reproach arose,
گفت با ما منشین کز تو سلامت برخاست
And said: "Sit not with me; for, from thee, safety hath risen.

که شنیدی که در این بزم دمی خوش بنشست
Of whom heardest thou (of the world), who at this banquet, hath awhile sat happy:
که نه در آخر صحبت به ندامت برخاست
Who, at the end of the companionship, not in remorse hath risen.

۱۹ تیر - July 10

هر که آمد به جهان نقش خرابی دارد
Whoever came to this (effacing) this world hath the mark of ruin the effacement by death, of this borrowed existence:

در خرابات بگویید که هشیار کجاست
In the tavern, (the world) ask ye saying: "The sensible one is where?"

آن کس است اهل بشارت که اشارت داند
One of glad tidings is he who knoweth the sign:

نکته‌ها هست بسی محرم اسرار کجاست
Many are the subtleties. The confidant of mysteries is where?

۲۰ تیر - July 11

مرو به خانه ارباب بی‌مروت دهر
Go not to the house of the Lords void of liberality of the age;

که گنج عافیتت در سرای خویشتن است
For the corner of ease in the dwelling of one's self is.

بسوخت حافظ و در شرط عشقبازی او
Hafez consumed; and (so consumed) in the condition of love and of life stakin

هنوز بر سر عهد و وفای خویشتن است
Yet, at the head of covenant and of fidelity of himself is

۲۱ تیر - July 12

هر که شد محرم دل در حرم یار بماند
Whoever became the confidant of his own he art, in the sacred fold of the (true) Beloved remained

وان که این کار ندانست در انکار بماند
He, who knew not this matter, in ignorance remained.

اگر از پرده برون شد دل من عیب مکن
If, forth from the screen, went my heart (abandoning outward reputation and choosing evilness) censure not:

شکر ایزد که نه در پرده پندار بماند
Thanks to God, that not, in the screen of thought (self-worshipping and pride), it remained.

۲۲ تیر - July 13

سینه مالامال درد است ای دریغا مرهمی
Alas full, full of pain is my heart, a plaister
دل ز تنهایی به جان آمد خدا را همدمی
God through loneliness, to (giving up) life my heart hath come; a companion

چشم آسایش که دارد از سپهر تیزرو
From the swift moving sky, hope of ease, hath who
ساقیا جامی به من ده تا بیاسایم دمی
O Saki a cup bring, so that I may rest a while.

۲۳ تیر - July 14

دیدی ای دل که غم عشق دگربار چه کرد
O heart! the grief of love, again, thou sawest what it did,
چون بشد دلبر و با یار وفادار چه کرد
When the heart-ravisher went; and with the beloved, fidelity-observing, what it did.

آه از آن نرگس جادو که چه بازی انگیخت
Alas! what play, (and calamities) that narcissus, the sorcerer, excited:
آه از آن مست که با مردم هشیار چه کرد
Alas! with men of sense (in making them senseless) that intoxicated, what it did.

۲۴ تیر - July 15

سایه معشوق اگر افتاد بر عاشق چه شد
If the (true) Beloved's shade fell on the lover, what
ما به او محتاج بودیم او به ما مشتاق بود
In need of Him, we are desirous of us, He was.

حسن مه رویان مجلس گر چه دل می‌برد و دین
Although the beauty of those moon of face of the assembly taketh heart and religion
بحث ما در لطف طبع و خوبی اخلاق بود
(Not on outward beauty, but) With the grace of temperament and with the beauty of disposition (of lovers) our love was.

۲۵ تیر - July 16

ببین که سیب زنخدان تو چه می‌گوید
Behold, what saith the apple of Thy chin!
هزار یوسف مصری فتاده در چه ماست
"Many a Yusuf of Egypt fallen into the pit, of ours is."

اگر به زلف دراز تو دست ما نرسد
If to our hand reach not Thy long tress,
گناه بخت پریشان و دست کوته ماست
The sin of the perturbed fortune, and of the short-hand of ours is.

۲۶ تیر - July 17

اشک من رنگ شفق یافت ز بی‌مهری یار
From the mercilessness of the beloved, my tears gained the colour of twilight:
طالع بی‌شفقت بین که در این کار چه کرد
In this work, (of love) behold my compassionless fortune what it did.

برق از منزل لیلی بدرخشید سحر
In the morning from Leyla's dwelling, lightning flashed;
وه که با خرمن مجنون دل افگار چه کرد
Alas! with the harvest (of existence) of Majnun, heart-rent what it did.

۲۷ تیر - July 18

جز این قدر نتوان گفت در جمال تو عیب
Of defect in thy beauty, one cannot speak save to this degree
که وضع مهر و وفا نیست روی زیبا را
That the way of love and of constancy belongeth not to the lovely face.

در آسمان نه عجب گر به گفته حافظ
On the sky, what if, of Hafez's utterances
سرود زهره به رقص آورد مسیحا را
Zuhra's[1] singing should bring to dancing the Masiha (Christ).

1-Refers to the planet Venus, the symbol of the beloved

۲۸ تیر - July 19

غرور حسنت اجازت مگر نداد ای گل
O rose (murshid, beautiful as the rose)! perhaps the pride of beauty hath not given thee permission

که پرسشی نکنی عندلیب شیدا را
That thou makest no inquiry as to the state (full of grief, void of hypocrisy) of the distraught nightingale (Hafiz).

به خلق و لطف توان کرد صید اهل نظر
By beauty of disposition, people of vision one can captivate:

به بند و دام نگیرند مرغ دانا را
Not by snare and net, take they the wise bird.

۲۹ تیر - July 20

رحم کن بر من مسکین و به فریادم رس
On me, miserable, show pity and to my plaint, arrive

تا به خاک در آصف نرسد فریادم
So that, to the dust of the door of Asaf, my plaint reach not.

حافظ از جور تو حاشا که بگرداند روی
Of thy tyranny, God forbid that Hafiz should, one day, complain

من از آن روز که دربند توام آزادم
From this day when, in thy bond, I am, free I am.

۳۰ تیر - July 21

زلف بر باد مده تا ندهی بر بادم
So that me, to the wind of destruction thou givenot, to the dishevelling breeze, thy tress givenot

ناز بنیاد مکن تا نکنی بنیادم
So that my foundation of life, thou take not, the foundation of disdain, establish not.

می مخور با همه کس تا نخورم خون جگر
So that (in affliction) the blood of my liver, I drinknot, with others, wine drink not

سر مکش تا نکشد سر به فلک فریادم
So that its head to the sky, my plaint draw not, thy head with draw not.

۳۱ تیر - July 22

به گوش هوش نیوش از من و به عشرت کوش
With the ear of sense, listen to me; and for ease, strive:
که این سخن سحر از هاتفم به گوش آمد
For, to my ear, from an invisible messenger, this matter of the morning came.

چه جای صحبت نامحرم است مجلس انس
The assembly of affection is the place of society of the excluded what!
سر پیاله بپوشان که خرقه پوش آمد
Cover the mouth of the cup; for the Khirka[1]-wearer (the Zahid) is came

---

1-Cloak

فصل تابستان
(Summer)

مرداد
August

۱ مرداد - July 23

روی تو کس ندید و هزارت رقیب هست
Thy face, none hath seen; and (yet) a thousand watchers are Thine,
در غنچه‌ای هنوز و صدت عندلیب هست
Still (hidden) in the (folded) rosebud, Thine many a nightingale is.

گر آمدم به کوی تو چندان غریب نیست
Not so strange is it if to Thy street came
چون من در آن دیار هزاران غریب هست
I, since in this country many a stranger (traveller) is.

۲ مرداد - July 24

پیر پیمانه کش من که روانش خوش باد
Our Pir[1], the wine-measurer whose soul be happy
گفت پرهیز کن از صحبت پیمان شکنان
Said: The society of covenant-breakers, shun.

دامن دوست به دست آر و ز دشمن بگسل
Into the hand, the Friend's skirt bring; from the enemy break away
مرد یزدان شو و فارغ گذر از اهرمنان
The man oi God, be by Ahriman[2], safely pass.

۳ مرداد - July 25

فرصت شمر طریقه رندی که این نشان
Reckon as plunder the path of profligacy. For this track,
چون راه گنج بر همه کس آشکاره نیست
Like the path to the (hidden) treasure, evident to everyone is not.

نگرفت در تو گریه حافظ به هیچ رو
In no way, Hafez's weeping affected thee
حیران آن دلم که کم از سنگ خاره نیست
Astonishment (is) mine at that heart, which less hard than the (hard) stone is not.

1-A Muslim saint or holy man, Pietist
2-Devil

July 26 - ۴ مرداد

آن که رخسار تو را رنگ گل و نسرین داد
Who, to thy cheek, the hue of the (red) rose and of the wild (white) rose gave,
صبر و آرام تواند به من مسکین داد
To me, miserable, patience and ease, can give.

وان که گیسوی تو را رسم تطاول آموخت
Who taught thy tress the habit of being long,
هم تواند کرمش داد من غمگین داد
To me, grief-stricken, the gift of His liberality, can also give.

July 27 - ۵ مرداد

آن که رخسار تو را رنگ گل و نسرین داد
Hope of Farhad, (that he would live) I severed that very day
که عنان دل شیدا به لب شیرین داد
When, to Shirin's lip, the rein of his distraught heart, he gave.

گنج زر گر نبود کنج قناعت باقیست
If (mine) be not the treasure of gold, contentment is left:
آن که آن داد به شاهان به گدایان این داد
Who, to kings that (treasure) gave, to beggars this (contentment) gave.

July 28 - ۶ مرداد

یاری اندر کس نمی‌بینیم یاران را چه شد
Friendship in none, I perceive. To friends what hath happened?
دوستی کی آخر آمد دوستداران را چه شد
Friendship ended when? To friends what hath happened?

آب حیوان تیره گون شد خضر فرخ پی کجاست
Black of hue became (the limpid, gleaming) the water of life. Khizr[1], auspicious of foot, is where?
خون چکید از شاخ گل باد بهاران را چه شد
From (its own roseate color, the rose hath changed). To the spring-breeze what hath happened?

1-Name of prophet

July 29 - ۷ مرداد

برو معالجه خود کن ای نصیحتگو
counsel utterer! (wine – forbidder) go, devise thy own remedy:
شراب و شاهد شیرین که را زیانی داد
Loss to whom, (is it that) wine and the sweet mistress gave.

گذشت بر من مسکین و با رقیبان گفت
By me miserable, He passed and told to my opponents:
دریغ حافظ مسکین من چه جانی داد
Alas What a soul, my slain lover gave.

July 30 - ۸ مرداد

مطرب عشق عجب ساز و نوایی دارد
Wonderful harmony and great melody, my minstrel of love hath:
نقش هر نغمه که زد راه به جایی دارد
Every picture of the hidden (divine knowledge) that he striketh, path to place hath.

عالم از ناله عشاق مبادا خالی
Void of the wailing of lovers, be not the world:
که خوش آهنگ و فرح بخش هوایی دارد
For a note, pleasant of melody and joy-giving, it hath.

July 31 - ۹ مرداد

آن که از سنبل او غالیه تابی دارد
That one, from whose (fragrant) hyacinth lock, a great torment, (of jealousy) ambergris hath.
باز با دلشدگان ناز و عتابی دارد
Again, with those heart-gone, (lovers) grace and reproach hath.

از سر کشته خود می گذری همچون باد
By the head of his own slain one, (the lover) He (the Beloved) passeth (swiftly) like the wind:
چه توان کرد که عمر است و شتابی دارد
What can one do? For, He is (like swift) life and swiftness (of departing) it (life) hath.

August 1 - ۱۰ مرداد

چنگ خمیده قامت می‌خواندت به عشرت
The harp, bent of form, calleth thee to joy:
بشنو که پند پیران هیچت زیان ندارد
Hearken: for any injury to thee, the counsel of old men hath not.

ای دل طریق رندی از محتسب بیاموز
O heart, learn the way of profligates from the Mohtaseb.
مست است و در حق او کس این گمان ندارد
Intoxicated, he is; yet of him this suspicion (of intoxication) any one hath not.

August 2 - ۱۱ مرداد

جان بی جمال جانان میل جهان ندارد
Without the (true) Beloved's beauty, inclination for the world, my soul hath not:
هر کس که این ندارد حقا که آن ندارد
O God, (I swear) everyone who this (the Beloved's beauty) hath not, that (the soul) hath not.

با هیچ کس نشانی زان دلستان ندیدم
A trace of that Heart-Ravisher, with none, I beheld:
یا من خبر ندارم یا او نشان ندارد
No news of him, have I: He, a trace hath not.

August 3 - ۱۲ مرداد

نیست بر لوح دلم جز الف قامت دوست
On my heart's table t is naught save the (straight) alif of the Friend's stature
چه کنم حرف دگر یاد نداد استادم
What may I do Me, recollection of other letter the teacher (the murshid) thee gave not.

کوکب بخت مرا هیچ منجم نشناخت
Recognised the star of my fortune, astrologer none
یا رب از مادر گیتی به چه طالع زادم
O Lord! of mother-earth, beneath what natal star, born was I!

August 4 - مرداد ۱۳

روشنی طلعت تو ماه ندارد
The luminosity of Thy face, the (resplendent) moon halt not:
پیش تو گل رونق گیاه ندارد
In comparison with Thee, the glory of (common) grass, the (splendid) rose hath not.

گوشه ابروی توست منزل جانم
The corner of Thy eye-brow is my soul's dwelling:
خوشتر از این گوشه پادشاه ندارد
More happy than this corner, the king hath not

August 5 - مرداد ۱۴

احوال گنج قارون کایام داد بر باد
The circumstances of the treasure of Qarun which, to the wind of destruction Time gave.
در گوش دل فروخوان تا زر نهان ندارد
Utter ye to (the rose-bud the miser) so that its gold, hidden, it have not

گر خود رقیب شمع است اسرار از او بپوشان
If the companion himself be the candle, from him conceal mysteries:
کان شوخ سربریده بند زبان ندارد
For that bold one, head severed, ligature (bridle) on his tongue, hath not.

August 6 - مرداد ۱۵

تو مگر بر لب آبی به هوس بنشینی
Perchance, with desire (of khilvat) by the marge of a pool, thou sittest (not),
ور نه هر فتنه که بینی همه از خود بینی
If not, every calamity, that (thou experiencest), all thou experiences from self-seeingness.

به خدایی که توئی بنده بگزیده او
(I conjure thee) by God, Whose chosen slave, thou art,
که بر این چاکر دیرینه کسی نگزینی
That, to this ancient slave, none thou choose (prefer)

۱۶ مرداد - August 7

هر چند پیر و خسته دل و ناتوان شدم
Although old, shattered of heart, powerless, I have become
هر گه که یاد روی تو کردم جوان شدم
Whenever I recollected Thy face, made, young I became.
شکر خدا که هر چه طلب کردم از خدا
Thanks to God that whatever, from God, I sought,
بر منتهای همت خود کامران شدم
To the limit of my spirit, prosperous I became.

۱۷ مرداد - August 8

گیسوی چنگ ببرید به مرگ می ناب
At the death of pure wine, sever the tress (cord) of the harp
تا حریفان همه خون از مژه‌ها بگشایند
So that, blood, from the eye-lashes, all the companions will loose.
در میخانه ببستند خدایا مپسند
O God they (fate and destiny) closed the door of the wine-house. Approve not
که در خانه تزویر و ریا بگشایند
For, the door of deception and of hyprocrisy, they will

۱۸ مرداد - August 9

سال‌ها دل طلب جام جم از ما می‌کرد
Search for the cup of Jamshid (divine knowledge) from me, (zahid and 'abid) years my heart made.
وان چه خود داشت ز بیگانه تمنا می‌کرد
And for what it (the cup) possessed, from a stranger, entreaty made.
گوهری کز صدف کون و مکان بیرون است
A jewel the (true Beloved) that is beyond the shell of existence and of time,
طلب از گمشدگان لب دریا می‌کرد
From those lost on the shore of the sea, (of unity) search it (my heart) made.

August 10 - مرداد ۱۹

به عزم مرحله عشق پیش نه قدمی
Advance a step for traveling to love's stage,
که سودها کنی ار این سفر توانی کرد
For, profits, thou mayst make if this journey thou canst make.

تو کز سرای طبیعت نمی‌روی بیرون
Thou that goest not forth from the house of nature (the body)
کجا به کوی طریقت گذر توانی کرد
How passage to the street of Tarikat, (is it that) thou canst make.

August 11 - مرداد ۲۰

ای پادشه خوبان داد از غم تنهایی
O king of the lovely (the beloved) ones of the world for grief of being alone, justice
دل بی تو به جان آمد وقت است که بازآیی
Without Thee, to the soul, my heart hath come. Tis the time when thou shouldst come back (and me safety, give).

دایم گل این بستان شاداب نمی‌ماند
(O Beloved) Ever joyous, remaineth not the rose of this garden (of the world).
دریاب ضعیفان را در وقت توانایی
At the time of power fulness (perfection of beauty) the feeble one aid (and their state, pity)

August 12 - مرداد ۲۱

گناه چشم سیاه تو بود و گردن دلخواه
The sin (fault) of Thy dark eye, and of Thy heart-alluring neck, it was,
که من چو آهوی وحشی ز آدمی برمیدم
That, like the wild deer, from man I fled.

چو غنچه بر سرم از کوی او گذشت نسیمی
Over my head, from His street, a (fragrant) breeze like (perfumed) the rose-bud passed
که پرده بر دل خونین به بوی او بدریدم
For (obtaining) the perfume of which, the screen over my poor heart, I rent.

August 13 - مرداد ۲۲

سال‌ها پیروی مذهب رندان کردم
Years, the pursuit of the service of profligates I made
تا به فتوی خرد حرص به زندان کردم
Until, by wisdom's decree, greed into prison, I put.

من به سرمنزل عنقا نه به خود بردم راه
Not of myself, took I the path to the abode of the (inaccessible) Anka[1] (the true Beloved)
قطع این مرحله با مرغ سلیمان کردم
With the bird of Sulaiman (the lapwing) the travelling of the stage, I made.

August 14 - مرداد ۲۳

سایه‌ای بر دل ریشم فکن ای گنج روان
O treasure of desire on my heart-wound, thy shade cast
که من این خانه به سودای تو ویران کردم
For, by exceeding desire for thee, this house (the heart) desolate, I made.

توبه کردم که نبوسم لب ساقی و کنون
I repented, saying: The Saki's lip J will not kiss. And now,
می‌گزم لب که چرا گوش به نادان کردم
My lip, I bite because my ear to the (counsel of the) foolish, I placed.

August 15 - مرداد ۲۴

ز دست کوته خود زیر بارم
Through my short (feeble) arm, beneath grief's load, am I
که از بالابلندان شرمسارم
For, of those of lofty stature ashamed, am I.

مگر زنجیر مویی گیردم دست
Perchance, my hand, the chain of the hair (of Thy tress) will take
وگر نه سر به شیدایی برآرم
If not, in distraughtness, my head I bring forth.

1-Phoenix

August 16 - ۲۵ مرداد

من پیر سال و ماه نیم یار بی‌وفاست
Not old in years and months, am I the faithless friend, it was,
بر من چو عمر می‌گذرد پیر از آن شدم
(Who, swiftly), like (swift) life, passeth by me from (grief of) that, old, I became

دوشم نوید داد عنایت که حافظا
Last night, me, glad tidings, he, (the Pir of the Magians, the perfect murshid) gave, saying Hafiz
بازآ که من به عفو گناهت ضمان شدم
Comeback; for the pardon of thy sins, surety I became.

August 17 - ۲۶ مرداد

دارم از لطف ازل جنت فردوس طمع
From (through) the grace of eternity without beginning, paradise, I greedily desire
گر چه دربانی میخانه فراوان کردم
Although, door-keeping of the wine-house, much I did.

این که پیرانه سرم صحبت یوسف بنواخت
This that the society of Yusuf (divine grace) cherisheth my elderly head
اجر صبریست که در کلبه احزان کردم
Is the reward of that patience that, in the sorrowful cell, I made.

August 18 - ۲۷ مرداد

هر می لعل کز آن دست بلورین ستدیم
Every red wine that, from that crystal (pure) hand (of the murshid), I took,
آب حسرت شد و در چشم گهربار بماند
Became the water of regret; and, in my eye, the jewel of (rain) tear remained.

جز دل من کز ازل تا به ابد عاشق رفت
Save my heart, that, from eternity without beginning to eternity without end, proceeded Thy lover,
جاودان کس نشنیدیم که در کار بماند
I have heard of none, whoever in the work (of being Thy lover) remained.

August 19 - مرداد ۲۸

ز چشم شوخ تو جان کی توان برد
(In safety) How can one take one's life from Thy bold eye,
که دایم با کمان اندر کمین است
That ever is in ambuscade with the bow?

بر آن چشم سیه صد آفرین باد
Be a hundred (shouts of) Afarin! on that dark eye,
که در عاشق کشی سحرآفرین است
Which, in lover-slaying is the creator of magic.

August 20 - مرداد ۲۹

امید در شب زلفت به روز عمر نبستم
Hope in the (dark) night of Thy (dark) tress for the bright day of life, I established not
طمع به دور دهانت ز کام دل ببریدم
From the heart's desire, desire for Thy mouth's round form, I severed

به شوق چشمه نوشت چه قطره‌ها که فشاندم
From desire for Thy sweet fountain, what drops were (tears they were) that I scattered
ز لعل باده فروشت چه عشوه‌ها که خریدم
From Thy ruby (lip) wine-selling, what graces I purchased

August 21 - مرداد ۳۰

صبح خیزی و سلامت طلبی چون حافظ
Morning-rising (open – heartedness) and salvation-seeking, like Hafiz
هر چه کردم همه از دولت قرآن کردم
Whatever I did, all from the fortune of the Kuran, I did.

گر به دیوان غزل صدرنشینم چه عجب
If in the Divan of ghazals[1] (the assembly, whereat songs they sing on) the chief seat, I sat, what wonder
سال‌ها بندگی صاحب دیوان کردم
Years, the service of the master of the Divan, I made.

1-Sonnet, ode

August 22 - ۳۱ مرداد

مرا می‌بینی و هر دم زیادت می‌کنی دردم
Me, Thou beholdest; and, in a moment, my pain, greater Thou makest

تو را می‌بینم و میلم زیادت می‌شود هر دم
Thee, I be hold and momently my inclination for Thee greater becometh.

به سامانم نمی‌پرسی نمی‌دانم چه سر داری
As to my state, Thou askest not what mystery Thou hast, I know not

به درمانم نمی‌کوشی نمی‌دانی مگر دردم
For my remedy, Thou strivest not perchance, my pain, Thou knowest not

فصل تابستان
(Summer)

شهریور
September

۱ شهریور - August 23

دوش با من گفت پنهان کاردانی تیزهوش
Last night, tome, a mystery-knower, keen of sense, secretly spake,
و از شما پنهان نشاید کرد سر می فروش
Saying Concealed from thee, one cannot hold the mystery of the wine-seller

گفت آسان گیر بر خود کارها کز روی طبع
He said To thy self, action easy take. For, from nature's way
سخت می‌گردد جهان بر مردمان سختکوش
On men hard striving, hard the world seizeth.

۲ شهریور - August 24

گر چه افتاد ز زلفش گرهی در کارم
Although, from His tress, a knot (of difficulty) hath fallen upon my work
همچنان چشم گشاد از کرمش می‌دارم
Even so, from His liberality, the solution (of it) I expect.

به طرب حمل مکن سرخی رویم که چو جام
To joy, the ruddiness of my face attribute not For, like the cup,
خون دل عکس برون می‌دهد از رخسارم
Forth from my cheek, the (ruddy) reflection, the heart's blood giveth.

۳ شهریور - August 25

منم آن شاعر ساحر که به افسون سخن
That poet-magician am I, who, with the sorcery of speech
از نی کلک همه قند و شکر می‌بارم
From the reed-pen, all candy and sugar, rain.

دیده بخت به افسانه او شد در خواب
By His tale, to sleep went fortune's eye
کو نسیمی ز عنایت که کند بیدارم
Where, a breeze of favour, that, me, awake may make?

۴ شهریور - August 26

زلفین سیاه تو به دلداری عشاق
For the consolation of lovers, Thy two tresses
دادند قراری و ببردند قرارم
A great covenant, gave; and my rest, took

ای باد از آن باده نسیمی به من آور
O breeze (murshid) me, a fragrant waft from that cup (of wine of divine love) bring
کان بوی شفابخش بود دفع خمارم
For, (from the grief of) wine-sickness (temptations of the world me) convalescence, that perfume (giveth).

۵ شهریور - August 27

در نهانخانه عشرت صنمی خوش دارم
In the secret house of my ease (the heart) a sweet idol (the true Beloved) I have
کز سر زلف و رخش نعل در آتش دارم
From Whose tress-tip and cheek, the horse-shoe (of agitation) in the fire I have

عاشق و رندم و میخواره به آواز بلند
With loud shout, me (they call) lover, profligate, wine-drinker
وین همه منصب از آن حور پریوش دارم
From that Hur[1], like the Pari[2], all I have

۶ شهریور - August 28

چراغ صاعقه آن سحاب روشن باد
Luminous be the lamp of lightning of that cloud
که زد به خرمن ما آتش محبت او
That, to our harvest (of existence) dashed the fire of love of His

بر آستانه میخانه گر سری بینی
If, on the threshold of the wine-house, a head thou see,
مزن به پای که معلوم نیست نیت او
With the foot, kick not. Not known, is the purpose of His

1-Lover
2-Beautiful woman

۷ شهریور - August 29

تا ابد بوی محبت به مشامش نرسد
To eternity without end, the perfume of (divine) love reacheth not the perfume place of him
هر که خاک در میخانه به رخساره نرفت
Who, with his face, swept not the dust of the door of the tavern (the stage of love and of divine knowledge).

سخن عشق نه آن است که آید به زبان
Not that which cometh to the tongue is the talk of love:
ساقیا می ده و کوتاه کن این گفت و شنفت
O Saki! (Murshid) give wine; make short this uttering and hearing of love.

۸ شهریور - August 30

تو همچو صبحی و من شمع خلوت سحرم
Like the morning (of laughing forehead) Thou art, and the candle of the chamber of the morning, I am
تبسمی کن و جان بین که چون همی‌سپرم
Smile and be hold how (for Thee) my soul, I surrender

چنین که در دل من داغ زلف سرکش توست
In my heart, the stain of (love for) Thy heart-alluring tress is so (in dwelling) that
بنفشه زار شود تربتم چو درگذرم
When (from this vanishing world) I pass, my tomb becometh the (dark) dark violet bed.

۹ شهریور - August 31

قدح پر کن که من در دولت عشق
Full, make the goblet for from love's fortune, I
جوان بخت جهانم گر چه پیرم
(Will make) youthful fortune (to leap), though old I am.

قراری بسته‌ام با می فروشان
With the wine-sellers, an arrangement I have made,
که روز غم بجز ساغر نگیرم
That, on grief's day, naught save the cup (of love) of I take.

۱۰ شهریور - September 1

به تیغم گر کشد دستش نگیرم
If, with the sword (of tyranny) He (the true Beloved) slay me, His hand, I seize not
وگر تیرم زند منت پذیرم
If, upon me, this arrow He strike, obliged I am.
کمان ابرویت را گو بزن تیر
To (the true Beloved) say (At that) our eye brow, Thy arrow strike,
که پیش دست و بازویت بمیرم
That, before Thy hand and arm, I may die.

۱۱ شهریور - September 2

چشمه چشم مرا ای گل خندان دریاب
O laughing rose! (the beloved) discover the fountain of my eye,
که به امید تو خوش آب روانی دارد
That, in hope of thee, a torrent of sweet water hath.
گوی خوبی که برد از تو که خورشید آن جا
From thee, who taketh the ball of beauty, when (even) the (refulgent) sun here
نه سواریست که در دست عنانی دارد
Is not a horseman, that in his hand, a rein (of choice) hath?

۱۲ شهریور - September 3

گر دست رسد در سر زلفین تو بازم
IF into the curl of Thy two tresses, my hand again should reach,
چون گوی چه سرها که به چوگان تو بازم
With Thy chaugan[1], what heads (there are) that like a ball, I shall play.
زلف تو مرا عمر دراز است ولی نیست
Long life to me is Thy (long) tress but there is not
در دست سر مویی از آن عمر درازم
In my hand, a hair-tip of this long life.

1-Polo Spor

۱۳ شهریور - September 4

چرا نه در پی عزم دیار خود باشم
In the pursuit of the desire of visiting my own (native) Land, why should I not be
چرا نه خاک سر کوی یار خود باشم
The dust of the head of my (true) Beloved's street, why should I not be

غم غریبی و غربت چو بر نمی‌تابم
When the load of grief of being a stranger and the trouble, I bear not,
به شهر خود روم و شهریار خود باشم
To my own city, I go and, my own monarch, I shall be.

۱۴ شهریور - September 5

هوای منزل یار آب زندگانی ماست
The air of the Friend's dwelling is our water of life,
صبا بیار نسیمی ز خاک شیرازم
O breeze from the dust of Shiraz, me, a fragrant perfume bring.

سرشکم آمد و عیبم بگفت روی به روی
Forth came my tear and told my crime face to face (publicly)
شکایت از که کنم خانگیست غمازم
Complaint may I make of whom of my house hold, the informer is.

۱۵ شهریور - September 6

بنما به من که منکر حسن رخ تو کیست
Show to me, the denier of the beauty of Thy face, who is he
تا دیده‌اش به گزلک غیرت برآورم
So that, with the dagger of jealousy, his eye I may bring forth.

بر من فتاد سایه خورشید سلطنت
On me, fell the shadow of the (symbolic) sun of empire
و اکنون فراغت است ز خورشید خاورم
Now, (as) to the (material) sun of the east, rest (independence) is mine.

۱۶ شهریور - September 7

در خرابات مغان گر گذر افتد بازم
If again be fall me passing into the tavern of the Magians (the perfect murshid)

حاصل خرقه و سجاده روان دربازم
The produce of the Khirka and of the prayer-mat, running (recklessly) I will play away (and lose)

حلقه توبه گر امروز چو زهاد زنم
If to-day, like the Zahids[1], I beat the ring of penitence,

خازن میکده فردا نکند در بازم
To-morrow, open to me the door, the wine-house-guardian maketh not.

۱۷ شهریور - September 8

پروانه راحت بده ای شمع که امشب
O candle (Beloved) give the order for rest. For, to-night,

از آتش دل پیش تو چون شمع گدازم
From the heart's fire, before Thee, like the consuming candle I melt.

آن دم که به یک خنده دهم جان چو صراحی
That moment when, with a laugh, life I give up like the flagon

مستان تو خواهم که گزارند نمازم
I would that a prayer for me Thy intoxicated ones should offer.

۱۸ شهریور - September 9

غم گیتی گر از پایم درآرد
If, me from off my feet, the world's grief bring,

بجز ساغر که باشد دستگیرم
Save the cup, my hand-seizer (helper) is who

برآی ای آفتاب صبح امید
O Sun of the morning of hope (the true Beloved) come forth

که در دست شب هجران اسیرم
For, in the hand of the (dark) night of separation, captive am I

1-Pietist

September 10 - شهریور ۱۹

مژده وصل تو کو کز سر جان برخیزم
Where, the glad tidings of union with Thee, so that, from desire of life, I may rise
طایر قدسم و از دام جهان برخیزم
The holy bird (of paradise) am I from the world's snare, I rise.

به ولای تو که گر بنده خویشم خوانی
By Thy love (I swear) that, if me, Thy slave, Thou call,
از سر خواجگی کون و مکان برخیزم
Out from desire of lord ship of existence and dwelling (both worlds) I rise.

September 11 - شهریور ۲۰

یا رب از ابر هدایت برسان بارانی
O Lord! from the cloud of guidance, the rain (of mercy) cause to arrive
پیشتر زان که چو گردی ز میان برخیزم
Before that, from the midst, like a (handful of) dust, I rise.

بر سر تربت من بی می و مطرب بنشین
(O holy traveller) At the head of my tomb, without wine and the minstrel, sit not
تا به بویت ز لحد رقص کنان برخیزم
So that by thy perfume, dancing, I may rise.

September 12 - شهریور ۲۱

به فریادم رس ای پیر خرابات
O Pir of the tavern (the murshid excellent and perfect) come to my cry (for justice)
به یک جرعه جوانم کن که پیرم
By a draught, me young make for old am I

به گیسوی تو خوردم دوش سوگند
Last night, by thy tress, I ate an oath,
که من از پای تو سر بر نگیرم
That, my head, from off thy foot, I will not take.

September 13 - ۲۲ شهریور

من دوستدار روی خوش و موی دلکشم
The friend I am of the sweet face; and of the heart-alluring hair:
مدهوش چشم مست و می صاف بی‌غشم
Distraught with the intoxicated. eye, I am and with pure unalloyed wine.

گفتی ز سر عهد ازل یک سخن بگو
Thou askedest Of the mystery of the covenant of eternity without beginning, say one word,
آن گه بگویمت که دو پیمانه درکشم
(I reply) That moment when two cups of wine, I drink, I will tell thee.

September 14 - ۲۳ شهریور

ز دست بخت گران خواب و کار بی‌سامان
Of the hand of fortune, heavy with sleep and of resourceless work,
گرم بود گله‌ای رازدار خود باشم
If complaint be mine, my own secret-keeper, I shall be.

همیشه پیشه من عاشقی و رندی بود
The being a lover and a profligate was ever my way
دگر بکوشم و مشغول کار خود باشم
Again, I will strive and engaged in my own work I shall be.

September 15 - ۲۴ شهریور

عمریست تا من در طلب هر روز گامی می‌زنم
Tis a life-time since, in search (of good fame) every day, a pace I cast:
دست شفاعت هر زمان در نیک نامی می‌زنم
Every moment, the hand of entreaty on good fame I cast.

بی ماه مهرافروز خود تا بگذرانم روز خود
Without my moon (the Beloved) love-kindling, let me see how my day I pass:
دامی به راهی می‌نهم مرغی به دامی می‌زنم
On a path, a net I lay a fowl in the snare, I cast.

۲۵ شهریور - September 16

من که از آتش دل چون خم می در جوشم
Although from the heart's fire, like a (foaming) jar of wine, in tumult I am,

مهر بر لب زده خون می‌خورم و خاموشم
The seal (of silence) on my lip pressed, the blood (of grief) I drink and silent I am.

قصد جان است طمع در لب جانان کردن
To show desire for the lip of the (true) Beloved is (to make) an attempt upon (one's own) life

تو مرا بین که در این کار به جان می‌کوشم
Be hold thou me who, in this matter, with soul (strenuously) strive

۲۶ شهریور - September 17

من آدم بهشتیم اما در این سفر
Adam of paradise, I am but in this journey (through this world)

حالی اسیر عشق جوانان مه وشم
Now, captive to the love of youthful ones (I am).

در عاشقی گزیر نباشد ز ساز و سوز
In being a lover (of God) is no escape from consuming and (yet) being content

استاده‌ام چو شمع مترسان ز آتشم
Like the candle, standing I am me of the fire (of love) affright not

۲۷ شهریور - September 18

هست امیدم که علیرغم عدو روز جزا
Hope is mine that despite the enemy (shaitan) on the day of requital (resurrection – day)

فیض عفوش ننهد بار گنه بر دوشم
Not, on my back, will the bounty of His pardon place the load of sin.

پدرم روضه رضوان به دو گندم بفروخت
For two wheat-grains, my Father (Adam) sold the garden of Rizvan (paradise)

من چرا ملک جهان را به جوی نفروشم
If, for a barley-grain, I sell it not, (un worthy son I shall be).

September 19 - شهریور ۲۸

حجاب چهره جان می‌شود غبار تنم
The dust of my body is the veil of the (true) Beloved's face
خوشا دمی که از آن چهره پرده برفکنم
O happy that moment when from off this face, the veil I cast

چنین قفس نه سزای چو من خوش الحانیست
Not fit for a sweet singer like me, is the cage (of the world) like this
روم به گلشن رضوان که مرغ آن چمنم
To Rizvan's rose-bed, I go for the bird of that sward am I

September 20 - شهریور ۲۹

شاه شوریده سران خوان من بی‌سامان را
Me, resourceless (of wisdom) king of those distraught of head, call
زان که در کم خردی از همه عالم بیشم
On that account that, in being one of little wisdom, greater than all the world I am.

بر جبین نقش کن از خون دل من خالی
(O true Beloved) On Thy forehead with my heart's blood, a great mole depict
تا بدانند که قربان تو کافر کیشم
So that they (men) may know that, sacrifice for Thee, kafir of religion, I am

September 21 - شهریور ۳۰

هزار جهد بکردم که یار من باشی
Efforts, a thousand, I made that my (true) Beloved, thou shouldst be.
مرادبخش دل بی‌قرار من باشی
(That) The desire-giver of my sorrowful heart, Thou shouldst be.

چراغ دیده شب زنده دار من گردی
(O true Beloved since) The lamp of my eye, Thou madest night a live keeper (watchful)
انیس خاطر امیدوار من باشی
The consoler of my hopeful heart, Thou shalt be.

۳۱ شهریور - September 22

اگر ز خون دلم بوی شوق می‌آید
If, from my heart's blood, the perfume of musk issue,
عجب مدار که همدرد نافه ختنم
Have no wonder for fellow-sufferer with the musk-pod of Khutan[1] (the musk – deer) I am.

طراز پیرهن زرکشم مبین چون شمع
(Outwardly) Regard not the embroidery of my gold-thread tunic (resplendent) like the candle, (saying He is happy)
که سوزهاست نهانی درون پیرهنم
For, within the tunic, hidden consuming sate.

1- A musk deer

فصل پاییز
(Autumn)

مهر
October

۱ مهر - September 23

سلامی چو بوی خوش آشنایی
A salutation, like the pleasant perfume of friendship
بدان مردم دیده روشنایی
To that man of the eye of light

درودی چو نور دل پارسایان
A salutation, like the light of the heart of the pious
بدان شمع خلوتگه پارسایی
To that candle of the khilvat[1]-place of piety

۲ مهر - September 24

سر ارادت ما و آستان حضرت دوست
(Together are) the head of our desire, and the threshold of the Mighty Friend (God):
که هر چه بر سر ما می‌رود ارادت اوست
For, whatever (of good, or of bad) passeth over our head is His will.

نظیر دوست ندیدم اگر چه از مه و مهر
My Friend's equal, I have not seen; although (the gleaming) of the moon and of the shining sun,
نهادم آینه‌ها در مقابل رخ دوست
The mirrors opposite to the Friend's face I placed.

۳ مهر - September 25

آن چه در مدت هجر تو کشیدم هیهات
In the time of separation from Thee, what I endured alas
در یکی نامه محال است که تحریر کنم
'Tis impossible that, in one letter, writing thereof I should make

با سر زلف تو مجموع پریشانی خود
With (on account) of Thy own tress-tip (is) all my perturbation
کو مجالی که سراسر همه تقریر کنم
Where the power that, all at once, all the narrative, I should make

---

1-Solitude

۴ مهر - September 26

بی تو ای سرو روان با گل و گلشن چه کنم

O morning cypress without thee, with the rose and the rose-bud, what may I do

زلف سنبل چه کشم عارض سوسن چه کنم

The tress of the hyacinth, how may I draw; (with) the cheek of the lily what may I do

آه کز طعنه بدخواه ندیدم رویت

From the reproach of the ill-wisher, alas I be held not Thy face

نیست چون آینه‌ام روی ز آهن چه کنم

When not mine is the (gleaming) mirror, with (dull) iron what may I do

۵ مهر - September 27

مایه خوشدلی آن جاست که دلدار آن جاست

There, where is the heart-possessor, is the source of happy-heartedness

می‌کنم جهد که خود را مگر آن جا فکنم

I strive that, perchance there, myself, I may cast.

بگشا بند قبا ای مه خورشیدکلاه

O moon, sun of cap (in effulgence) the fastening of thy coat, loose

تا چو زلفت سر سودازده در پا فکنم

So that like thy (long, trailing) tress at thy feet, my passion-stricken head I may cast

۶ مهر - September 28

واعظ ما بوی حق نشنید بشنو کاین سخن

Perceived not truth's perfume, our admonisher. Hear thou for this word (of

در حضورش نیز می‌گویم نه غیبت می‌کنم

In his presence, do I also utter no calumny, do I make.

با صبا افتان و خیزان می‌روم تا کوی دوست

To the Friend's street, I go like the (swift) breeze, falling and rising,

و از رفیقان ره استمداد همت می‌کنم

And from (the basil and the rose), prayer for assistance, I make.

September 29 - ۷ مهر

من ترک عشق شاهد و ساغر نمی‌کنم
Love for the lovely one and for the cup, I abandon not.
صد بار توبه کردم و دیگر نمی‌کنم
A hundred times, repentance, I made, (and broke it) again (repentance) I make not.

باغ بهشت و سایه طوبی و قصر و حور
The garden of paradise, the shade of the Tuba tree, and the palace of the Hur
با خاک کوی دوست برابر نمی‌کنم
Equal (even) to the dust of the Friend's street, 'I make not.

September 30 - ۸ مهر

گر از این منزل ویران به سوی خانه روم
If, from this stage of (this world) travel towards the house (my native land, the next world) I go
دگر آن جا که روم عاقل و فرزانه روم
When there again I go, wise and learned, I go

زین سفر گر به سلامت به وطن بازرسم
If, from this journey, in safety to my native land, I return,
نذر کردم که هم از راه به میخانه روم
I vow that, by the way to the wine-house (of love) I go

October 1 - ۹ مهر

ناگهان پرده برانداخته‌ای یعنی چه
(O beloved) suddenly, thy veil thou up-castedest. This is what?

مست از خانه برون تاخته‌ای یعنی چه
Intoxicated, forth from the house, thou hastenedest. This is what?

زلف در دست صبا گوش به فرمان رقیب
In the power of the breeze, thy tress (thou hast given) to the order of the watcher, thy ear (thou hast placed)
این چنین با همه درساخته‌ای یعنی چه
Thus, with all thou hast contented thy self. This is what.

۱۰ مهر - October 2

گرم از دست برخیزد که با دلدار بنشینم
If, from my hand, there arise (the chance) that with my heart-possessor I may sit,

ز جام وصل می‌نوشم ز باغ عیش گل چینم
From the cup of fortune (of His face) I drink, (wine and) from the garden of union (with Him) pluck the rose (of profit)

شراب تلخ صوفی سوز بنیادم بخواهد برد
(Not) My foundation (of life) will the bitter (strong) wine (real love) sufi-consuming take

لبم بر لب نه ای ساقی و بستان جان شیرینم
O Saki (perfect murshid)! on my lip, thy lip, place; and my sweet life, take.

۱۱ مهر - October 3

در خرابات مغان نور خدا می‌بینم
In the tavern of the Magians, God's light I see

این عجب بین که چه نوری ز کجا می‌بینم
This wonder be hold what the light (is and) where it, I see.

جلوه بر من مفروش ای ملک الحاج که تو
O King (commander) of the Hajj to me, boast not of dignity. For, thou

خانه می‌بینی و من خانه خدا می‌بینم
Seest the house (the Ka'ba) and God's house, I see.

۱۲ مهر - October 4

بیا با ما مورز این کینه داری
(O beloved) Come towards us this hatred exercise not

که حق صحبت دیرینه داری
For the light of ancient society, thou hast.

نصیحت گوش کن کاین در بسی به
My counsel hear for this pearl (of counsel) much better is

از آن گوهر که در گنجینه داری
Than that jewel that, in the treasury, thou hast.

October 5 - ۵ مهر - ۱۳

به مژگان سیه کردی هزاران رخنه در دینم
A thousand breaches in my faith, with Thy dark eye-lashes,
Thou hast made:
بیا کز چشم بیمارت هزاران درد برچینم
Come, so that, out (of my heart) on account of Thy sick (languishing) eye, a thousand pains, (of mine) I may pluck.

الا ای همنشین دل که یارانت برفت از یاد
Ho, O fellow-sitter, of my heart (the true Beloved) from Whose memory, friends (who, in this world of non-existence are Thy companions and slumber in Thy unity) have passed
مرا روزی مباد آن دم که بی یاد تو بنشینم
Not a day be mine, the moment when, void of recollection of Thee, I sit.

October 6 - ۶ مهر - ۱۴

دیدار شد میسر و بوس و کنار هم
Obtained was the sight of (the true Beloved) and the kiss, and the embrace also
از بخت شکر دارم و از روزگار هم
To fortune, thanks I owe and to time, also.

زاهد برو که طالع اگر طالع من است
Zahid go (about thy own work and forbid not wine and the lovely one) For if ascendant be my fortune,
جامم به دست باشد و زلف نگار هم
Will be in my hand, the cup and the Beloved's tress also

October 7 - ۷ مهر - ۱۵

دردم از یار است و درمان نیز هم
From the (true) Beloved, is my pain and my remedy, also
دل فدای او شد و جان نیز هم
A sacrifice for Him, became my heart, and my life, also

این که می‌گویند آن خوشتر ز حسن
Those that say That (elegance) is better than beauty (To them, say)
یار ما این دارد و آن نیز هم
This (beauty) hath our Beloved and that (elegance) also

October 8 - ۱۶ مهر

ما بدین در نه پی حشمت و جاه آمده‌ایم
Not in pursuit of pomp and of pageant, to this door (of the murshid) we have come
از بد حادثه این جا به پناه آمده‌ایم
For shelter from ill-fortune, here we have come.
ره رو منزل عشقیم و ز سرحد عدم
Way-farers of love's stage are we and from the limits of non-existence,
تا به اقلیم وجود این همه راه آمده‌ایم
Up to the climes of existence, all this way we have come.

October 9 - ۱۷ مهر

بعد صد سال اگر بر سر خاکم گذری
If, after a hundred years, Thy (perfume) blow over my dust,
سر برآرد ز گلم رقص کنان عظم رمیم
Forth from the clay (of the grave) its head the rotten bone dancing bringeth
دلبر از ما به صد امید ستد اول دل
First, from us, with a hundred hopes, the Heart-Ravisher took our heart
ظاهرا عهد فرامش نکند خلق کریم
Apparently, the covenant, His merciful nature forgetteth not.

October 10 - ۱۸ مهر

روز هجران و شب فرقت یار آخر شد
"The day of separation from, and the night of disunion with, the (true) Beloved is ended:"
زدم این فال و گذشت اختر و کار آخر شد
This omen, I cast; the star (of happy omen) passed; and the work of grief is ended.
آن همه ناز و تنعم که خزان می‌فرمود
All that grace and beauty, (of snare) that autumn (the world) displayed,
عاقبت در قدم باد بهار آخر شد
At last, at the foot of the (arrival of) spring-breeze, (the murshid) is ended.

۱۹ مهر - October 11

حسن تو همیشه در فزون باد
Ever increasing, Thy beauty be!
رویت همه ساله لاله گون باد
All years, tulip-hued, Thy face be.

اندر سر ما خیال عشقت
In my head, the image of Thy love,
هر روز که باد در فزون باد
Every day that is, increasing be.

۲۰ مهر - October 12

صلاح از ما چه می‌جویی که مستان را صلا گفتیم
From us, where fore seeketh thou peace, when, to the intoxicated, an invitation we uttered
به دور نرگس مستت سلامت را دعا گفتیم
At the revolution of thy intoxicated eye, fare well to safety we uttered.

در میخانه‌ام بگشا که هیچ از خانقه نگشود
Open me the door of the wine-house (of love and drink wine that divine mysteries may be revealed to thee) for, from the monastery, naught is revealed
گرت باور بود ور نه سخن این بود و ما گفتیم
If thine be belief (of my word) if not, this was the speech, we uttered

۲۱ مهر - October 13

ای باد اگر به گلشن احباب بگذری
O breeze! if thou pass by the rose-bed of beloved ones,
زنهار عرضه ده بر جانان پیام ما
Take care! present to the beloved (the murshid) the message of ours.

گو نام ما ز یاد به عمدا چه می‌بری
(O breeze!) From thy memory, our name why purposely takest thou?
خود آید آن که یاد نیاری ز نام ما
Itself (forgetfulness) cometh, when (after death) cometh no recollection of ours.

October 14 - ۲۲ مهر

بیا تا گل برافشانیم و می در ساغر اندازیم

(O murshid) come so that the rose (of ease and of pleasure) we may scatter, and, into the cup (of existence or of the heart) the wine (of love and of divine knowledge) cast,

فلک را سقف بشکافیم و طرحی نو دراندازیم

(By our inward strength) the roof of the sky we rend and (to the height of another heaven) a new way, cast.

اگر غم لشکر انگیزد که خون عاشقان ریزد

If an army, that sheddeth the blood of lovers, grief raise

من و ساقی به هم تازیم و بنیادش براندازیم

Content to get her are I and the Saki and up its foundation, we cast.

October 15 - ۲۳ مهر

ما نگوییم بد و میل به ناحق نکنیم

Evil (of any) we utter not inclination of any to the in justice (of any) we make not

جامه کس سیه و دلق خود ازرق نکنیم

Black, (the face of) any one and blue, our own religious garment, we make not,

عیب درویش و توانگر به کم و بیش بد است

Evil, it is (to show) in deficiency or in excess the defect of the poor man, or of the rich man

کار بد مصلحت آن است که مطلق نکنیم

The counsel is that evil work at all, we do not.

October 16 - ۲۴ مهر

دوستان وقت گل آن به که به عشرت کوشیم

Friends in the rose-season, that best that "for pleasure we strive"

سخن اهل دل است این و به جان بنیوشیم

(This) the word of (the Pir of the Magians the murshid) the is. With soul, let us listen.

نیست در کس کرم و وقت طرب می‌گذرد

In none, is liberality (that we may have even a groat wherewith to drink wine) passeth joy's time

چاره آن است که سجاده به می بفروشیم

Its remedy is this, for wine, the prayer-mat, we sell.

۲۵ مهر - October 17

با مدعی مگویید اسرار عشق و مستی
To the adversary, utter not the mysteries of love and of intoxication,
تا بی‌خبر بمیرد در درد خودپرستی
So that, without knowledge (of love) in pain of self-worshipping, he may die

عاشق شو ار نه روزی کار جهان سر آید
(O Zahid) The lover (of the true Beloved) be if not, one day, the world's work endeth
ناخوانده نقش مقصود از کارگاه هستی
(And) from the workshop of existence (the world) the picture of thy purpose unread (unattained, thou shall die)

۲۶ مهر - October 18

می‌سوزم از فراقت روی از جفا بگردان
(O beloved) from separation from thee, I consume
هجران بلای ما شد یا رب بلا بگردان
Separation (from the beloved) our (soul)-calamity became O Lord! the calamity,

مه جلوه می‌نماید بر سبز خنگ گردون
On the bay courser of the sky, the moon displayeth splendour:
تا او به سر درآید بر رخش پا بگردان
So that, to an end, it may come, to (mighty) Rakhsh[1], thy foot turn.

۲۷ مهر - October 19

ای نور چشم مستان در عین انتظارم
O light of the eye of the intoxicated in the essence of expectation, I am
چنگ حزین و جامی بنواز یا بگردان
The wailing harp and the cup, (that one, the harp) play and the (this one, the cup) beturn

دوران همی‌نویسد بر عارضش خطی خوش
When, on thy cheek, time writeth the happy line,
یا رب نوشته بد از یار ما بگردان
O Lord! from our friend, the ill-decree, turn.

1-The name of horse

October 20 - ۲۸ مهر

آن ترک پری چهره که دوش از بر ما رفت
That Bold One of Angel-face (the true Beloved) who, last night, by me passed,
آیا چه خطا دید که از راه خطا رفت
What sin saw He that, by way of sin, He passed?
تا رفت مرا از نظر آن چشم جهان بین
Since from my sight, went that world-seeing eye,
کس واقف ما نیست که از دیده چه‌ها رفت
None knoweth what tears from my eye have passed.

October 21 - ۲۹ مهر

خدا را کم نشین با خرقه پوشان
(O true Beloved) For God's sake, with Khirka[1]-wearers (hypocrites) little sit
رخ از رندان بی‌سامان مپوشان
From resource less profligates (inwardly pure and clean) Thy face, conceal not

در این خرقه بسی آلودگی هست
In this Khirka (of the austere zahids) is many a stain
خوشا وقت قبای می فروشان
O happy the time of the kaba[2] of the wine-drinkers (void of stain)

October 22 - ۳۰ مهر

شاه شمشادقدان خسرو شیرین دهنان
The Shah of those box-tree of stature, Khusrau of those sweet of mouth,
که به مژگان شکند قلب همه صف شکنان
Who, with His eye-lash, the center (of an army) all rank-shatterers, shattereth,
مست بگذشت و نظر بر من درویش انداخت
Passed intoxicated and, on me, the dervish, a glance cast
گفت ای چشم و چراغ همه شیرین سخنان
(And) Said eye and lamp of those all sweet of speech

1-Cloak
2-Long garment

فصل پاییز
(Autumn)

آبان
November

October 23 - ۱ آبان

چشم خود را گفتم آخر یک نظر سیرش ببین
To my eye, I spake saying At last, Him once fully be hold
گفت می‌خواهی مگر تا جوی خون راند ز من
It (the eye) said Perchance thou wishest that a stream of blood should pour from me.

او به خونم تشنه و من بر لبش تا چون شود
Thirsty for my blood, He and for, (His blood) I So that when it happeneth,
کام بستانم از او یا داد بستاند ز من
My desire I will take from Him; or justice (revenge) He will take from me.

October 24 - ۲ آبان

نکته‌ای دلکش بگویم خال آن مه رو ببین
A heart-alluring subtlety, I utter, the mole of that one moon of face, be hold.
عقل و جان را بسته زنجیر آن گیسو ببین
Bound with the chain of that tress, my reason and soul be hold

عیب دل کردم که وحشی وضع و هرجایی مباش
My heart, I censured, saying: One of bestial, or one of desert, nature, be not;
گفت چشم شیرگیر و غنج آن آهو ببین
It said The eye (half intoxicated of) the bold one of that deer (the true Beloved) be hold

October 25 - ۳ آبان

از چشم بخت خویش مبادت گزند از آنک
From the (evil) eye-, (wound of the people) no injury be thine (for).
در دلبری به غایت خوبی رسیده‌ای
To exceeding beauty in heart-ravishing ness, thou hast attained

منعم مکن ز عشق وی ای مفتی زمان
Their garment of patience, thou hast rent
معذور دارمت که تو او را ندیده‌ای
I hold the excused for her thou hast not seen.

October 26 - ۴ آبان

وصال او ز عمر جاودان به
Union with (the Beloved) than ever lasting life, better
خداوندا مرا آن ده که آن به
O Lord! me that (union) give for that (is) best.

به شمشیرم زد و با کس نگفتم
Me, with the sword, He struck and to none, I spake
که راز دوست از دشمن نهان به
For, concealed from the enemy, the Beloved's mystery best.

October 27 - ۵ آبان

کنار آب و پای بید و طبع شعر و یاری خوش
The water-bank, and the willow-root and the poetic nature and a friend, happy
معاشر دلبری شیرین و ساقی گلعذاری خوش
A companion, the sweet heart-ravisher, and the Saki, rose of cheek, happy

الا ای دولتی طالع که قدر وقت می‌دانی
Ho! O fortune of destiny that knoweth (not) the worth of time,
گوارا بادت این عشرت که داری روزگاری خوش
To thee, be this pleasure pleasant for a time, thou hast happy.

October 28 - ۶ آبان

مزرع سبز فلک دیدم و داس مه نو
The green expanse of sky, I be held and the sickle (the crescent) of the new moon
یادم از کشته خویش آمد و هنگام درو
To me, recollection came of my owns own-field and of the time of reaping (the judgment – day)

گفتم ای بخت بخفتیدی و خورشید دمید
I said fortune thou hast slept and appeared hath the sun
گفت با این همه از سابقه نومید مشو
He said Despite all this, hopeless of the past, be not.

October 29 - ۷ آبان

بشنو این نکته که خود را ز غم آزاده کنی

This my subtlety, hear that, free from grief, thyself thou mayst make

خون خوری گر طلب روزی ننهاده کنی

Blood (of grief) thou drinkest, if search for victuals, not placed (intended for thee) thou makest.

آخرالامر گل کوزه گران خواهی شد

In the end, the clay of the goglet-maker (potters) thou wilt become;

حالیا فکر سبو کن که پر از باده کنی

Now, think of the pitcher (of thy heart) that, it, full of wine (of ma'rifat and of love) thou mayst make

October 30 - ۸ آبان

محروم اگر شدم ز سر کوی او چه شد

If, from the head of His street, I am excluded, what matter

از گلشن زمانه که بوی وفا شنید

From the rose-bed of Time, the perfume of fidelity, who perceived

ساقی بیا که عشق ندا می‌کند بلند

Saki come For love maketh high clamour,

کان کس که گفت قصه ما هم ز ما شنید

Saying That one who uttered our tale, even from us heard.

October 31 - ۹ آبان

دوش رفتم به در میکده خواب آلوده

Last night, to the door of the wine-house, I went, sleep stained

خرقه تر دامن و سجاده شراب آلوده

The Khirka wet of skirt, and the prayer-mat, wine stained

آمد افسوس کنان مغبچه باده فروش

Them again boy of the wine-seller, cry-making, came

گفت بیدار شو ای ره رو خواب آلوده

He said Awake, O way farer, sleep stained.

November 1 - ۱۰ آبان

آن آهوی سیه چشم از دام ما برون شد
Forth from our snare, that mistress, dark of eye, hath gone
یاران چه چاره سازم با این دل رمیده
Friends what remedy may I make with this heart affrighted
زنهار تا توانی اهل نظر میازار
Take care so far as thou canst, injure not people of vision
دنیا وفا ندارد ای نور هر دو دیده
No fidelity, hath the world. O light of both eyes

November 2 - ۱۱ آبان

از آن رنگ رخم خون در دل افتاد
For that colour of face, He (God) cast into my heart the blood (of grief)
و از آن گلشن به خارم مبتلا کرد
And from this rose-bed (eternity without beginning) entangled in the thorn (of the world with a thousand afflictions) me made.
غلام همت آن نازنینم
I am the slave of resolution of that graceful one, (the true Beloved)
که کار خیر بی روی و ریا کرد
Who, without dissimulation and hypocrisy, the work of liberality made.

November 3 - ۱۲ آبان

آن که فکرش گره از کار جهان بگشاید
To that one, whose thought looseneth the knot (of difficulty) the world's work,
گو در این کار بفرما نظری بهتر از این
Say In this (subtlety of love) make (reflection) better than this.
ناصحم گفت که جز غم چه هنر دارد عشق
Tome, the admonisher spoke, saying: Save grief, what specialty hath love
برو ای خواجه عاقل هنری بهتر از این
(I said) O wise Khwaja[1] (it hath) ask ill better than this.

1--Eunuch, dignitary, vizier, boss, host

November 4 - آبان ۱۳

لبش می‌بوسم و در می‌کشم می
His lip, I kiss and down drink its wine
به آب زندگانی برده‌ام پی
To the water of life I have taken my foot.

نه رازش می‌توانم گفت با کس
Neither His mystery can I utter to any
نه کس را می‌توانم دید با وی
Nor anyone can I see (in comparison) with Him.

November 5 - آبان ۱۴

میل من سوی وصال و قصد او سوی فراق
My inclination, towards Union; and His towards separation:
ترک کام خود گرفتم تا برآید کام دوست
(Helpless) I abandoned my own desire that there might issue the desire of the Friend.

حافظ اندر درد او می‌سوز و بی‌درمان بساز
Hafez! In grief for Him, continue to consume; remediless, be content.
زان که درمانی ندارد درد بی‌آرام دوست
on that account, that no remedy hath the restless pain of the Friend

November 6 - آبان ۱۵

مخمور جام عشقم ساقی بده شرابی
O Saki intoxicated with love's cup, I am; give a little wine.
پر کن قدح که بی می مجلس ندارد آبی
Full, make the goblet for, without wine, the assembly hath not (even) a little luster

وصف رخ چو ماهش در پرده راست ناید
(Love for) His face like the moon, cometh not truly within the screen
مطرب بزن نوایی ساقی بده شرابی
Minstrel a melody, strike up Saki give a little wine.

November 7 - ۱۶ آبان

ای که بر ماه از خط مشکین نقاب انداختی
O thou that, on the moon (of thy radiant face) the veil of musky hair castest,

لطف کردی سایه‌ای بر آفتاب انداختی
Kindness, thou didst on the sun (thy effulgent face, so that from love's fire, lovers should not consume) a shade thou castest.

تا چه خواهد کرد با ما آب و رنگ عارضت
With us, the water (lustre of) colour of thy cheek, what will it do?

حالیا نیرنگ نقشی خوش بر آب انداختی
Now, on water, the picture of thy own sorcery, thou castest.

November 8 - ۱۷ آبان

ای دل مباش یک دم خالی ز عشق و مستی
O heart a moment, void of love and of intoxication, be not

وان گه برو که رستی از نیستی و هستی
At that time, go when, from non-existence to existence, thou escapedest.

گر جان به تن ببینی مشغول کار او شو
If (the Khirka-wearer), thou see, engaged in thy own work be

هر قبله‌ای که بینی بهتر ز خودپرستی
Every kibla[1] that (is) better than self-worshiping (is)

November 9 - ۱۸ آبان

دیدم به خواب دوش که ماهی برآمدی
Last night, in sleep, I saw that forth, a great moon had come

کز عکس روی او شب هجران سر آمدی
From the reflection of the face whereof, to an end, the night of separation had come.

تعبیر رفت یار سفرکرده می‌رسد
The explanation is what The much journeyed Friend (the true Beloved) arriveth

ای کاج هر چه زودتر از در درآمدی
O would (that) by my door, He, (splendour-giving, adorned), had come

---

1- direction to mohammadans turn which in praying.

November 10 - ۱۹ آبان

قلم را آن زبان نبود که سر عشق گوید باز
Not that tongue is the reed's that love's (great) mystery it may unfold
ورای حد تقریر است شرح آرزومندی
Beyond the limit of narration, is the explanation of longing.
الا ای یوسف مصری که کردت سلطنت مغرور
Ho O Yusuf of Egypt (the beloved) whom sovereignty (of Egypt) kept engaged
پدر را بازپرس آخر کجا شد مهر فرزندی
Ask the father, (Yakub) where went at last filial

November 11 - ۲۰ آبان

مرو چو بخت من ای چشم مست یار به خواب
O intoxicated eye of the beloved to sleep, like my fortune, go not
که در پی است ز هر سویت آه بیداری
For, in pursuit, from every direction, is the sigh of a wakeful one
نثار خاک رهت نقد جان من هر چند
The scattering of Thy Path's dust is my soul's cash, although
که نیست نقد روان را بر تو مقداری
On Thy part the soul's cash hath not (even) a little value.

November 12 - ۲۱ آبان

تو را که هر چه مراد است در جهان داری
(O Beloved) Thou whose purpose in the world whatever it be, Thou hast;
چه غم ز حال ضعیفان ناتوان داری
Of the state of the feeble (and of) the powerless, what grief (is it that) Thou hast
بخواه جان و دل از بنده و روان بستان
From Thy slave, life and heart, demand the soul, take
که حکم بر سر آزادگان روان داری
For over the free, the current order Thou hast

97

November 13 - ۲۲ آبان

ای که در کوی خرابات مقامی داری
O thou that, in the tavern-street, thy dwelling hast
جم وقت خودی ار دست به جامی داری
The Jamshid[1] of thy own time, thou art, if, on the cup, thy hand thou hast

ای که با زلف و رخ یار گذاری شب و روز
O thou that, night and day, with the tress and the face of the Beloved, passest
فرصتت باد که خوش صبحی و شامی داری
Be opportunity thine, so that a happy morning and evening thou mayst have.

November 14 - ۲۳ آبان

ای مگس حضرت سیمرغ نه جولانگه توست
O (contemptible) fly the presence of the (mighty) Simurgh is not thy place of display
عرض خود می‌بری و زحمت ما می‌داری
Thy own honour, thou takest and, our trouble, thou causest.

تو به تقصیر خود افتادی از این در محروم
Excluded from this door (of the true Beloved) by thy own fault, thou fellest,
از که می‌نالی و فریاد چرا می‌داری
Of whom, be wailest thou complaint, where fore (is it that) thou hast

November 15 - ۲۴ آبان

در ره منزل لیلی که خطرهاست در آن
In the path to the Abode of Laila (the true Beloved) where in are dangers,
شرط اول قدم آن است که مجنون باشی
The first condition of its step is, that Majnun (the perfect lover) the thou be.

نقطه عشق نمودم به تو هان سهو مکن
Thee, love's center I showed. Ho! mistake make not
ور نه چون بنگری از دایره بیرون باشی
If not, when thou lookest outside of the circle (of lovers) thou art

---

1- king

November 16 - ۲۵ آبان

می ده که گر چه گشتم نامه سیاه عالم
Wine, give. For, though black of book of the world, I became
نومید کی توان بود از لطف لایزالی
Hopeless of the grace of the Eternal, when can one be.

ساقی بیار جامی و از خلوتم برون کش
Saki a cup bring and, me, forth from khilvat put
تا در به در بگردم قلاش و لاابالی
So that, crafty and nothing-earning, door to door, I may wander.

November 17 - ۲۶ آبان

آسایش دو گیتی تفسیر این دو حرف است
The ease of two worlds (this and the next) is the explanation of these two words:
با دوستان مروت با دشمنان مدارا
With friends, kindness; with enemies, courtesy.

در کوی نیک نامی ما را گذر ندادند
In the street of good name outward rectitude they Fate and Destiny gave us no admission
گر تو نمی‌پسندی تغییر کن قضا را
If thou approve not, change our Fate.

November 18 - ۲۷ آبان

ای دل آن دم که خراب از می گلگون باشی
O heart that moment when, intoxicated with wine rose of hue, thou art
بی زر و گنج به صد حشمت قارون باشی
Without gold and treasure, with a hundred pomps of Karun thou art

در مقامی که صدارت به فقیران بخشند
In the stage where to fakirs the seat of wazirship, they give,
چشم دارم که به جاه از همه افزون باشی
I expect that above all in rank thou art.

November 19 - ۲۸ آبان

بگرفت کار حسنت چون عشق من کمالی
As my love (so) the work of Thy beauty took a great perfection
خوش باش زان که نبود این هر دو را زوالی
Happy be on this account that, this (beauty of love and of form) hath not (even) a little decline.

در وهم می‌نگنجد کاندر تصور عقل
In my imagination, it cometh not that in the (vain) imaginings of wisdom,
آید به هیچ معنی زین خوبتر مثالی
In any way, should come more beautiful than this a form.

November 20 - ۲۹ آبان

خمی که ابروی شوخ تو در کمان انداخت
The great curve that, into the bow, (of thy eye-brow), thy told eye-brow cast,
به قصد جان من زار ناتوان انداخت
In design of the blood of me, miserable, powerless, it cast.

نبود نقش دو عالم که رنگ الفت بود
Not the picture (of existence) of the two worlds was, when was the color of love:
زمانه طرح محبت نه این زمان انداخت
Not at this time, Love's foundation, did Time cast.

November 21 - ۳۰ آبان

بده ساقی می باقی که در جنت نخواهی یافت
Saki! give the wine (of divine love) remaining (from the people of religion); for, in Paradise, thou wilt not have
کنار آب رکن آباد و گلگشت مصلا را
The bank of the water of the Ruknabad (the lover's weeping eye) nor the rose of the garden of Musalla (the lover's heart).

فغان کاین لولیان شوخ شیرین کار شهرآشوب
Alas! These saucy dainty ones (lovely women) sweet of work, the torment of the city,
چنان بردند صبر از دل که ترکان خوان یغما را
Take patience from the heart even as the men of Turkistan (take) the tray of plunder.

فصل پاییز
(Autumn)
آذر
December

November 22 - آذر ۱

گر از آن آدمیانی که بهشتت هوس است
If, of those men thou be, whose desire is paradise,
عیش با آدمی ای چند پری زاده کنی
O Pari-born ease with man, how long (is it that) thou makest
تکیه بر جای بزرگان نتوان زد به گزاف
On the (sitting)-place of the great, boastingly it is impossible to lean,
مگر اسباب بزرگی همه آماده کنی
Unless, the chattels of greatness, all prepared, thou makest.

November 23 - آذر ۲

شد حظ عمر حاصل گر زان که با تو ما را
Life's delight would have been gained, if, with Thee, for us,
هرگز به عمر روزی روزی شود وصالی
Ever in life (only) one day had been the lot of a great union.
آن دم که با تو باشم یک سال هست روزی
That moment when, with Thee, I may be, the space of one (long) year is (only) a short day
وان دم که بی تو باشم یک لحظه هست سالی
That moment when, without Thee, I may be (the momentary twinkling of the eye) is a long year.

November 24 - آذر ۳

تا بی سر و پا باشد اوضاع فلک زین دست
Since, in this way, headless and footless (fickle) are the sky's motions,
در سر هوس ساقی در دست شراب اولی
In the head, desire for the Saki[1]; in the hand, wine best.
از همچو تو دلداری دل برنکنم آری
From a heart-possessor like thee, the heart up I pluck not. Yes
چون تاب کشم باری زان زلف به تاب اولی
If I endure torment, at least in the curl of that tress, best.

1- Tapster

November 25 - ۴ آذر

که برد به نزد شاهان ز من گدا پیامی
From me, the beggar, to kings, who taketh a message,
که به کوی می فروشان دو هزار جم به جامی
Saying: "In the street of the wine-sellers, (they sell) two thousand (mighty) Jamshids for a single cup of wine."

شده‌ام خراب و بدنام و هنوز امیدوارم
Ruined and ill of fame, I have become yet, hope I have
که به همت عزیزان برسم به نیک نامی
That, by the blessing of dear ones (those of good name) I may (escape from ill-fame and) reach to good-fame

November 26 - ۵ آذر

تا کی غم دنیای دنی ای دل دانا
O wise heart grief for a mean world, how long
حیف است ز خوبی که شود عاشق زشتی
Alas it is that with beauteousness, it (the heart) became the lover of hideousness

آلودگی خرقه خرابی جهان است
The stain of the Khirka is the ruin of the world
کو راهروی اهل دلی پاک سرشتی
Away-farer, one of heart, one pure of nature where

November 27 - ۶ آذر

سر خدمت تو دارم بخرم به لطف و مفروش
Desire for Thy service, I have; in kindness, me, purchase and sell not
که چو بنده کمتر افتد به مبارکی غلامی
For, into good fortune, seldom falleth, like (me) the slave a slave.

به کجا برم شکایت به که گویم این حکایت
My plaint, I take to where. This tale, I utter to whom
که لبت حیات ما بود و نداشتی دوامی
For thy lip was our life and, Thou hadst not (even) a little permanency.

۷ آذر - November 28

گر ز مسجد به خرابات شدم خرده مگیر

If from the Masjed[1] (outward worship) to the tavern (of truth) I go, carp not:

مجلس وعظ دراز است و زمان خواهد شد

Long is the assembly of admonition; (of the Zahid) and (short) the time (of life) shall be.

ای دل ار عشرت امروز به فردا فکنی

O heart! if to to-morrow thou cast (postpone) the joy of to-day,

مایه نقد بقا را که ضمان خواهد شد

Surety for the capital of cash of permanency, (till to – morrow) who shall be?

۸ آذر - November 29

وقت را غنیمت دان آن قدر که بتوانی

Time consider plunder to that degree that thou canst

حاصل از حیات ای جان این دم است تا دانی

O soul the out-come of life is (only) this moment if thou knowest.

کام بخشی گردون عمر در عوض دارد

The desire-giving of the sphere hath life in barter,

جهد کن که از دولت داد عیش بستانی

Strive that, from fortune, the justice of ease thou mayst take.

۹ آذر - November 30

پند عاشقان بشنو و از در طرب بازآ

The counsel of lovers, hear and out from the door of joy come

کاین همه نمی‌ارزد شغل عالم فانی

For all this is not worth the occupation of a transitory world.

پیش زاهد از رندی دم مزن که نتوان گفت

Before the Zahid, boast not of profligacy For one cannot utter

با طبیب نامحرم حال درد پنهانی

To the physician, not the confidant, the state of a hidden pain

---

1-Mosque

December 1 - ۱۰ آذر

هواخواه توام جانا و می‌دانم که می‌دانی
O (true) Beloved Thy well-wisher, I am, and (this) I know that Thou knowest
که هم نادیده می‌بینی و هم ننوشته می‌خوانی
For, both the un-seen, Thou seest; and also the un-written (by fate) Thou readest.
ملامتگو چه دریابد میان عاشق و معشوق
Of the mystery of the lover and of the Beloved, what gaineth the reproacher
نبیند چشم نابینا خصوص اسرار پنهانی
The non-seeing eye especially seeth not a secret mystery.

December 2 - ۱۱ آذر

خوش آمد گل وز آن خوشتر نباشد
Happy came the rose; and more happy than that aught is not.
که در دستت بجز ساغر نباشد
For, in thy hand, save the cup (of wine) aught is not.
زمان خوشدلی دریاب و در یاب
Gain, gain, the time of happy heartedness (leisure):
که دایم در صدف گوهر نباشد
For, in the shell, ever the jewel (wine in the cup, or concordant time) is not.

December 3 - ۱۲ آذر

ای که در کشتن ما هیچ مدارا نکنی
O thou who, in our slaughter, mercy exercisest not
سود و سرمایه بسوزی و محابا نکنی
Profit and capital, thou consumest manliness, thou showest not.
دردمندان بلا زهر هلاهل دارند
Deadly poison, the sorrowful ones of calamity (lovers, sorrowful through separation from thee) drink
قصد این قوم خطا باشد هان تا نکنی
The design of (slaying) this tribe (of lovers) is dangerous. Take care that it, thou doest not!

December 4 - ۱۳ آذر

رنج ما را که توان برد به یک گوشه چشم
Since, with a corner of thy eye, our grief it is possible to take
شرط انصاف نباشد که مداوا نکنی
The part of justice it is not, that our remedy (for freedom from grief) thou makest not.

دیده ما چو به امید تو دریاست چرا
Since, in hope of thee, our eye is the ocean (through weeping) why (is it that)
به تفرج گذری بر لب دریا نکنی
On the ocean-shore, in recreation, passing thou makest not

December 5 - ۱۴ آذر

خوش است خلوت اگر یار یار من باشد
Pleasant is Khalvat[1], if my beloved, the (true) Beloved shall be
نه من بسوزم و او شمع انجمن باشد
Not (pleasant) if I consume and the candle of (another) assembly, He shall be

من آن نگین سلیمان به هیچ نستانم
As naught, I take (regard) Sulaiman's seal-ring (the world's power),
که گاه گاه بر او دست اهرمن باشد
On which, sometimes, Ahriman's hand shall be.

December 6 - ۱۵ آذر

هر آن که کنج قناعت به گنج دنیا داد
Everyone who, for the world's treasure, gave the treasure of contentment,
فروخت یوسف مصری به کمترین ثمنی
Sold, (the precious) Yusuf of Egypt for a very paltry sum.

بیا که رونق این کارخانه کم نشود
Come; for not less becometh the amplitude of this workshop (the world)
به زهد همچو تویی یا به فسق همچو منی
By the austerity of one like thee or, by the profligacy of one like me.

1-Solitude

December 7 - ۱۶ آذر

کی شعر تر انگیزد خاطر که حزین باشد
How a (lustrous) verse exciteth afresh the heart that is sorrowful!
(through love for, and through the stain of, the world and from search after lust)

یک نکته از این معنی گفتیم و همین باشد
A subtlety out of this book, we uttered; and (enough) is this very subtlety.

از لعل تو گر یابم انگشتری زنهار
(O beloved)! if, from thy ruby (lip) I gain a ring of protection,

صد ملک سلیمانم در زیر نگین باشد
Beneath the order of my seal-ring, will be a hundred countries of Soleiman.

December 8 - ۱۷ آذر

باورم نیست ز بدعهدی ایام هنوز
After this, with the drum and the harp, to the wine - house I go

قصه غصه که در دولت یار آخر شد
For, in union with the true Beloved, the tale of grief of separation is ended.

ساقیا لطف نمودی قدحت پری باد
O Saki! thou showedest kindness. Be thy goblet full wine!

که به تدبیر تو تشویش خمار آخر شد
For, by thy deliberation, the disquietude of wine-sickness is ended.

December 9 - ۱۸ آذر

بیان شوق چه حاجت که سوز آتش دل
What need of the description of (love's) desire, when the explanation of the heart's fire,

توان شناخت ز سوزی که در سخن باشد
One can recognize from the burning which in speech may be.

هوای کوی تو از سر نمی‌رود آری
From our head, the desire for Thy street goeth not,

غریب را دل سرگشته با وطن باشد
With his native land, the stranger's distraught heart shall be.

December 10 - ۱۹ آذر

نفس باد صبا مشک فشان خواهد شد
Musk-diffusing, the breath of the morning breeze shall be:
عالم پیر دگرباره جوان خواهد شد
Again the world old (by autumn and winter) young shall be.

ارغوان جام عقیقی به سمن خواهد داد
To the (white) lily, the (ruddy) Arghavan[1] shall give the (red) cornelian cup
چشم نرگس به شقایق نگران خواهد شد
Glancing at the anemones, the eye of the narcissus shall be.

December 11 - ۲۰ آذر

بنشین بر لب جوی و گذر عمر ببین
On the marge of the (passing) stream, sit and the passing of life, be hold
کاین اشارت ز جهان گذران ما را بس
For this example of the passing world is for us enough.

نقد بازار جهان بنگر و آزار جهان
The cash of the world's market, and the world's pain, be hold
گر شما را نه بس این سود و زیان ما را بس
If this profit is not for you enough this loss, for us enough.

December 12 - ۲۱ آذر

ستاره‌ای بدرخشید و ماه مجلس شد
The star (Muhammad) gleamed; and the moon of the assembly (of the world) became:
دل رمیده ما را رفیق و مونس شد
Of our affrighted heart, the consoler and comforter became.

نگار من که به مکتب نرفت و خط ننوشت
My idol, (Muhammad) who to school went not; and writing wrote not:
به غمزه مسله آموز صد مدرس شد
With a glance, the precept-teacher of a hundred schools became.

1-Flower

December 13 - ۲۲ آذر

در نمازم خم ابروی تو با یاد آمد
When, in prayer, to me recollection of the curve of Thy eyebrow came.
حالتی رفت که محراب به فریاد آمد
(Over me such) a state passed that, into lament, the prayer-arch came.

از من اکنون طمع صبر و دل و هوش مدار
Now from me expect neither patience nor the heart of sense;
کان تحمل که تو دیدی همه بر باد آمد
For that patience, that thou sawest, to the wind all came.

December 14 - ۲۳ آذر

این شرح بی‌نهایت کز زلف یار گفتند
This endless explanation of the Beloved's beauty, that they (men of knowledge) uttered,
حرفیست از هزاران کاندر عبارت آمد
Is only a word out of thousands, that, into example, came.

عیبم بپوش زنهار ای خرقه می آلود
O thou wine-stained of garment! Take care; conceal my defect:
کان پاک پاکدامن بهر زیارت آمد
For, to visit me, that one pure of skirt (the true Beloved) came.

December 15 - ۲۴ آذر

گل عزیز است غنیمت شمریدش صحبت
Precious is the rose; its society reckon plunder.
که به باغ آمد از این راه و از آن خواهد شد
For in this way to the garden it came; and, (quickly) in that way shall go.

مطربا مجلس انس است غزل خوان و سرود
O minstrel! the assembly of associate friends, it is singing the ghazal and the ode:
چند گویی که چنین رفت و چنان خواهد شد
How long sayest thou: (This moment) "Passed like this; and like that shall be."

December 16 - ۲۵ آذر

امروز جای هر کس پیدا شود ز خوبان
The place (rank) of every one of the lovely ones (the beloved ones) becometh known to-day,

کان ماه مجلس افروز اندر صدارت آمد
When, to the chief seat, that moon, assembly-adorning, came.

بر تخت جم که تاجش معراج آسمان است
On the throne of Jam, whose crown is the (lofty) sun's ladder of ascen

همت نگر که موری با آن حقارت آمد
Behold the spirit! Notwithstanding (all) this contemptibility, a (feeble) ant (man) came.

December 17 - ۲۶ آذر

مکش آن آهوی مشکین مرا ای صیاد
O hunter (death) slay not that musky deer (the beloved)

شرم از آن چشم سیه دار و مبندش به کمند
Have shame of that dark (piteous) eye and, in the noose, bind him not.

من خاکی که از این در نتوانم برخاست
I, dusty, who, from this door (of separation from the Beloved) cannot rise

از کجا بوسه زنم بر لب آن قصر بلند
How may I plant a kiss on the lip of that lofty palace

December 18 - ۲۷ آذر

به روز واقعه تابوت ما ز سرو کنید
In the day of events (of death) make ye our coffin of the (lofty) cypress,

که می‌رویم به داغ بلندبالایی
For, we go with the mark of a lofty one.

زمام دل به کسی داده‌ام من درویش
My heart's rein I, the darvlsh, have given to that one (God)

که نیستش به کس از تاج و تخت پروایی
To whom, for any one's crown, or throne, is not (even) a little solicitude.

December 19 - ۲۸ آذر

گر می فروش حاجت رندان روا کند
If lawful the need of profligates, the wine-seller maketh,
ایزد گنه ببخشد و دفع بلا کند
His sin, God forgiveth; and, repelling of calamity maketh.
ساقی به جام عدل بده باده تا گدا
Saki! Give wine in the cup of justice, so that the beggar
غیرت نیاورد که جهان پر بلا کند
Gather not jealousy (such) that, the world full of calamity, he maketh.

December 20 - ۲۹ آذر

دوش گفتم بکند لعل لبش چاره من
Last night, (to my heart) I said: "Maketh the ruby of His lip my remedy?"
هاتف غیب ندا داد که آری بکند
Voice, gave the invisible messenger saying: "Yes! it maketh."
کس نیارد بر او دم زند از قصه ما
To Him, of our tale (of love) none can utter;
مگرش باد صبا گوش گذاری بکند
Perchance, its reporting the morning breeze maketh.

December 21 - ۳۰ آذر

جام می و خون دل هر یک به کسی دادند
The cup of wine (of ease) and the blood of the heart (of grief) each, they (Fate and Destiny) gave to each one:
در دایره قسمت اوضاع چنین باشد
In the action of destiny's circle, thus it is. (to one grief, to another ease)
در کار گلاب و گل حکم ازلی این بود
In the matter of rose-water and of the rose, the decree of eternity without beginning was this:
کاین شاهد بازاری وان پرده نشین باشد
"That (the rose) should be the lovely one of the bazar (the harlot); and that this (the rose – water) should be the sitter behind the veil." (the chaste one)

فصل زمستان (Winter)

دی
January

۱ دی - December 22

سحرم دولت بیدار به بالین آمد
In the morning, to my pillow, vigilant fortune came:
گفت برخیز که آن خسرو شیرین آمد
(And) said: (From sleep) Arise! For that thy dear Khosro (the true Beloved) hath come.

قدحی درکش و سرخوش به تماشا بخرام
"A goblet drink; (and), for seeing Him, merry of head, go:
تا ببینی که نگارت به چه آیین آمد
"That thou mayst see in what fashion, thy idol hath come.

۲ دی - December 23

نه هر که چهره برافروخت دلبری داند
Not every beloved ofle that up-kindleth his face the work of a heart-ravisher knoweth.
نه هر که آینه سازد سکندری داند
Not everyone who maketh the mirror (of Sikandar), the work of a Eskandar knoweth.

نه هر که طرف کله کج نهاد و تند نشست
Not everyone who slantwise placed his cap and sat severe
کلاه داری و آیین سروری داند
The work of a crown-possessor, and the usage of a Ruler knoweth.

۳ دی - December 24

رسید مژده که ایام غم نخواهد ماند
Arrived the glad tidings that grief's time shall not remain:
چنان نماند چنین نیز هم نخواهد ماند
Like that (joy's time) remained not; like this (grief's time) shall not remain.

من ار چه در نظر یار خاکسار شدم
Although, (by the ill-speaking of the watcher) I am, in the Beloved's sight, become dusty and despicable;
رقیب نیز چنین محترم نخواهد ماند
Honored like this, the watcher shall not remain.

۴ دی - December 25

من اگر کامروا گشتم و خوشدل چه عجب
If I became desire-gainer and happy of heart, what wonder?
مستحق بودم و اینها به زکاتم دادند
Deserving, I was; and me, these as alms they gave.

هاتف آن روز به من مژده این دولت داد
That day, me glad tidings of this fortune the invisible messenger gave:
که بدان جور و جفا صبر و ثباتم دادند
That in respect to that violence and tyranny, me, patience and endurance they gave.

۵ دی - December 26

گشت بیمار که چون چشم تو گردد نرگس
That, like Thy eye, it might become, the narcissus became sick (with futile effort):
شیوه تو نشدش حاصل و بیمار بماند
Its (Thy eye's) habit was not gained by it; and, sick, it remained.

از صدای سخن عشق ندیدم خوشتر
More pleasant than the sound of love's speech, naught I heard:
یادگاری که در این گنبد دوار بماند
(Twas) A great token, that, in this revolving dome remained.

۶ دی - December 27

بس تجربه کردیم در این دیر مکافات
In this house of retribution the upspringing of the world,
با دردکشان هر که درافتاد برافتاد
With the dreg-drunkards, (holy men) whoever in (strife) fell, out (in wretchedness) hath fallen.

گر جان بدهد سنگ سیه لعل نگردد
If the (valueless) black stone give (its own) life, it becometh not valuable the ruby:
با طینت اصلی چه کند بدگهر افتاد
What may it do? With its original (ill) nature, it, (the state of) ill-nature hath befallen.

December 28 - ۷ دی

حالیا مصلحت وقت در آن می‌بینم
Now, the good counsel of the time I see in that
که کشم رخت به میخانه و خوش بنشینم
That, to the wine-house, my chattels I be take and happy sit.

جام می گیرم و از اهل ریا دور شوم
The cup of wine, I take and, from the hypocrite, far I go
یعنی از اهل جهان پاکدلی بگزینم
That is, of the world's creation, (only), pureness of heart, I choose.

December 29 - ۸ دی

دوش وقت سحر از غصه نجاتم دادند
Last night, at morning time, me freedom from grief, they (Fate and Destiny) gave
واندر آن ظلمت شب آب حیاتم دادند
And, in that darkness of night, me the water-of-life they gave.

بیخود از شعشعه پرتو ذاتم کردند
Through the effulgence of the ray of His essence, me senseless, (and full of love for Him) they made:
باده از جام تجلی صفاتم دادند
(In the world) From the cup of splendor of His qualities, me wine they gave.

December 30 - ۹ دی

من که عیب توبه کاران کرده باشم بارها
I who, years, censured the repenters (of wine – drinking)
توبه از می وقت گل دیوانه باشم گر کنم
Repentance of (drinking) wine in the rose-season mad shall I be, if I make.

عشق دردانه‌ست و من غواص و دریا میکده
The (precious) pearl-grain is love I (am) the diver the wine-house (is) the sea
سر فروبردم در آن جا تا کجا سر برکنم
There, my head, I plunged (it) up-lifted, let us see, where shall I make

December 31 - ۱۰ دی

دلا دایم گدای کوی او باش
O heart be ever a beggar of His street
به حکم آن که دولت جاودان به
By the decree Perpetual fortune best

جوانا سر متاب از پند پیران
O youth from the counsel of old men, turn not thy head
که رای پیر از بخت جوان به
For, the old man's counsel than youthful fortune, better.

January 1 - ۱۱ دی

نرگس مست نوازش کن مردم دارش
The intoxicated narcissus, ('the beloved's eye), favor-doer, man-preserver;
خون عاشق به قدح گر بخورد نوشش باد
If it (the narcissus) drink lover's blood in a goblet, to it sweet may it be!

به غلامی تو مشهور جهان شد حافظ
Hafez! in thy service, the world became famous:
حلقه بندگی زلف تو در گوشش باد
In its ear, the ring of service of thy tress, be!

January 2 - ۱۲ دی

دوش دیدم که ملایک در میخانه زدند
Last night (in the hidden world) I saw that the angels beat (the world of love) (at) the door of the tavern,
گل آدم بسرشتند و به پیمانه زدند
(Whence they brought out moulds of love) The clay of Adam, they shaped and into the mould (of love), they cast.

ساکنان حرم ستر و عفاف ملکوت
The dwellers of the sacred fold of the veiling and of the abstaining (from what is forbidden) of the angels,
با من راه نشین باده مستانه زدند
On me, dust-sitter, (holy traveller) the intoxicating wine (of divine knowledge) cast.

January 3 - ۱۳ دی

نظر کردن به درویشان منافی بزرگی نیست
To glance at dervishes is not against greatness
سلیمان با چنان حشمت نظرها بود با مورش
With all his pomp, Sulaiman, his (mercy) glance was with the (feeble) ant

کمان ابروی جانان نمی‌پیچد سر از حافظ
From Hafiz, turneth not its head the bow of the eye-brow of the (true) Beloved
ولیکن خنده می‌آید بدین بازوی بی زورش
But, at this His arm full of force, (to Hafiz) laughter cometh.

January 4 - ۱۴ دی

دلا بسوز که سوز تو کارها بکند
O heart! Consume. For deeds (of God) thy consuming maketh:
نیاز نیم شبی دفع صد بلا بکند
The repelling of a hundred calamities, the midnight supplication maketh.

عتاب یار پری چهره عاشقانه بکش
The reproach of the (true) Beloved, Angel of face, endure like a lover:
که یک کرشمه تلافی صد جفا بکند
Because, compensation for a hundred (acts) of tyranny, one glance maketh.

January 5 - ۱۵ دی

کلک مشکین تو روزی که ز ما یاد کند
One day, when recollection of us thy musky reed maketh,
ببرد اجر دو صد بنده که آزاد کند
It (the reed) will take reward: Two hundred slaves that free, it maketh_

قاصد منزل سلمی که سلامت بادش
The messenger of Her Highness Salma-to whom be safety
چه شود گر به سلامی دل ما شاد کند
What is it if, with a (kind) salutation, our heart joyous, she maketh?

January 6 - ۱۶ دی

زاهد از کوچهٔ رندان به سلامت بگذر
O Zahed! Pass from the circle of profligates to safety:
تا خرابت نکند صحبت بدنامی چند
Lest ruined make thee, the society of some ill of fame.

عیب می جمله چو گفتی هنرش نیز بگو
The defect of wine, all thou toldest; its profit also tell:
نفی حکمت مکن از بهر دل عامی چند
Negation of (God's) skill make not for the sake of the heart of some people.

January 7 - ۱۷ دی

مقام امن و می بی‌غش و رفیق شفیق
The abode of peace, unalloyed wine, and the kind companion,
گرت مدام میسر شود زهی توفیق
If ever attainable these be to thee, O excellent the grace of God

جهان و کار جهان جمله هیچ بر هیچ است
The world and the world's work, all naught in naught is
هزار بار من این نکته کرده‌ام تحقیق
The verifying of this matter, a thousand times, I have made.

January 8 - ۱۸ دی

پشمینه پوش تندخو از عشق نشنیده‌است بو
(O Murshid) The wool-wearer, sullen of disposition (the hypocrite, captive to lust, in whom love hath no part) hath not perceived love's perfume:
از مستیش رمزی بگو تا ترک هشیاری کند
Of (its) loves intoxication, utter a hint, that, abandonment of sensibleness (and the choosing of the intoxication of love) he may make.

چون من گدای بی‌نشان مشکل بود یاری چنان
A beggar, void of mark, like me! A Friend (God) like that was difficult to obtain:
سلطان کجا عیش نهان با رند بازاری کند
Hidden pleasure with the common bazar-haunter, where doth the (great) Soltan make?

January 9 - ۱۹ دی

کی بود در زمانه وفا جام می بیار
In time, fidelity was where The cup of wine, bring,
تا من حکایت جم و کاووس کی کنم
That the tale of Jam[1], (and of) Kavus, and of, Kay[2], I may make.

از نامه سیاه نترسم که روز حشر
The black book (of sins) I fear not. for, in the day of assembling,
با فیض لطف او و صد از این نامه طی کنم
By the bounty of His grace, a hundred books of this kind, I would close.

January 10 - ۲۰ دی

از این سموم که بر طرف بوستان بگذشت
From this simum (blast of lust) that, by the garden-borders, passed
عجب که بوی گلی هست و رنگ نسترنی
Wonder that (from the heart of love's lust) the colour of a rose remaineth, or the perfume of a jessamine.

به صبر کوش تو ای دل که حق رها نکند
O heart strive thou for patience. For God delivereth not
چنین عزیز نگینی به دست اهرمنی
A seal-ring so precious (as patience) to the hand of an evil one.

January 11 - ۲۱ دی

دانی که چنگ و عود چه تقریر می کنند
Thou knowest what tale (it is) that the harp and the lyre (renowned men of piety) make?
پنهان خورید باده که تعزیر می کنند
Secretly drink ye wine (of love and reveal it not) that thee precious they may make.

ناموس عشق و رونق عشاق می برند
The honor of love and the splendor of lovers, they take:
عیب جوان و سرزنش پیر می کنند
The censure of the young; and the reproof of the old, they make.

1-Referring to Jamshid, a legendary ruler of ancient Iran
2-king

January 12 - ۲۲ دی

بود آیا که در میکده‌ها بگشایند
(O heart) It may be that the door of the wine-houses, they will open
گره از کار فروبسته ما بگشایند
The knot (of difficulty) of our entangled work they will open

اگر از بهر دل زاهد خودبین بستند
If, for the sake of the Zahid's heart, self-seeing, they closed the door
دل قوی دار که از بهر خدا بگشایند
Strong keep the heart; for, for the sake of God they will open

January 13 - ۲۳ دی

آنان که خاک را به نظر کیمیا کنند
Those (Mursheds)[1], who, (from exceeding firmness) with their glance alchemy of the dust (of the traveller's existence) make,
آیا بود که گوشه چشمی به ما کنند
At us, eye-cornering, (oblique glancing) do they make?

دردم نهفته به ز طبیبان مدعی
My pain concealed from the claimant's physician, best:
باشد که از خزانه غیبم دوا کنند
It may be that, its remedy from the treasury of the hidden, they (Fate and Destiny) make.

January 14 - ۲۴ دی

زاهد خلوت نشین دوش به میخانه شد
Last night, to the wine-house, (the Arif, the comprehender of truths) Zahed, sitting in khalwat[2], went:
از سر پیمان برفت با سر پیمانه شد
From the head of his covenant, he departed; (and) to the head of the cup, went.

صوفی مجلس که دی جام و قدح می‌شکست
Yesterday, the distraught Sufi who broke the cup and the goblet:
باز به یک جرعه می عاقل و فرزانه شد
Yester-night, by one draught of wine, (of love) wise and learned became.

1- Guru, mentor, spiritual guide, or preceptor
2- solitude

January 15 - ۲۵ دی

فی الجمله اعتماد مکن بر ثبات دهر
In short, on Time's permanency, rely not:
کاین کارخانه‌ایست که تغییر می‌کنند
For this (world) is the workshop wherein change they make

می خور که شیخ و حافظ و مفتی و محتسب
Drink wine. For the Shaikh[1], and Hafez, and the Mufti[2] and the Mohtaseb[3]
چون نیک بنگری همه تزویر می‌کنند
All when thou lookest well fraud (openly abstaining from wine, secretly drinking wine) make.

January 16 - ۲۶ دی

گر رنج پیش آید و گر راحت ای حکیم
Sage! If before thee come sorrow or ease,
نسبت مکن به غیر که اینها خدا کند
Ascribe not to other; (than God) for these, God maketh.

در کارخانه‌ای که ره عقل و فضل نیست
In the workshop, wherein is no path to reason and excellence,
فهم ضعیف رای فضولی چرا کند
An arrogant judgment, why (is it that) weak imagination maketh?

January 17 - ۲۷ دی

هر آن کسی که در این حلقه نیست زنده به عشق
In this circle, everyone who is not alive with love
بر او نمرده به فتوای من نماز کنید
Over him, not dead, by my decree, prayer for the dead make ye.

وگر طلب کند انعامی از شما حافظ
If from you, Hafiz demand a great reward
حوالتش به لب یار دلنواز کنید
To the lip of the Beloved, heart-cherishing, consignment of him make ye

---

1-Preacher
2-Lawyer
3-Sheriff

January 18 - ۲۸ دی

خیال روی تو در هر طریق همره ماست
In every path of Islam, the image of Thy face fellow traveler of ours is.
نسیم موی تو پیوند جان آگه ماست
Ever, the perfume of Thy hair, the soul-informer of ours is.
به رغم مدعیانی که منع عشق کنند
In grief of those claimants, who forbid love,
جمال چهره تو حجت موجه ماست
The beauty of Thy face, the approved argument of ours is.

January 19 - ۲۹ دی

در نظربازی ما بی‌خبران حیرانند
Astonished at our glance-playing, (in love's path) those voids of vision (the men of shara') are:
من چنینم که نمودم دگر ایشان دانند
As I appeared (infidel, or lover of God) so I am; the rest, they know.

عاقلان نقطه پرگار وجودند ولی
The sages are the center of the compass of existence; but
عشق داند که در این دایره سرگردانند
Love knoweth that, in this circle (of love), they head-revolving (their learning in love's path being useless) are.

January 20 - ۳۰ دی

گفتم کی ام دهان و لبت کامران کنند
I said: (O Beloved) "Me, prosperous, Thy mouth and lip, when do they make?"
گفتا به چشم هر چه تو گویی چنان کنند
He said: "By my eye (I swear that) whatever thou sayest even so do they make."

گفتم خراج مصر طلب می‌کند لبت
I said: "Thy lip (from exceeding sweetness) demandeth tribute of Egypt (sugar): "
گفتا در این معامله کمتر زیان کنند
He said: "In this matter, loss they seldom make."

فصل زمستان
(Winter)

بهمن
February

January 21 - ۱ بهمن

قتل این خسته به شمشیر تو تقدیر نبود
By the sword (of inclination) of thine, the slaughter of this shattered one decreed, it was not
ور نه هیچ از دل بی‌رحم تو تقصیر نبود
If not, (by the glance of sorcery of) thine, a fault it was not.

من دیوانه چو زلف تو رها می‌کردم
(O true Beloved) When I, distraught, released Thy tress
هیچ لایقترم از حلقه زنجیر نبود
For me, (distraught) more fit than the chain-fetter, aught was not

January 22 - ۲ بهمن

گر مدد خواستم از پیر مغان عیب مکن
If, from the wine-house, seek blessing, carp not
شیخ ما گفت که در صومعه همت نبود
Our Pir spake saying In the Christian cloister, blessing is not

چون طهارت نبود کعبه و بتخانه یکیست
When there is no purity (of heart from infidelity) one are the Ka'ba[1] and the idol house
نبود خیر در آن خانه که عصمت نبود
Well, it is not when, in the house (of the heart) chastity is not

January 23 - ۳ بهمن

ای گدایان خرابات خدا یار شماست
O beggars of the tavern! God is your Friend,
چشم انعام مدارید ز انعامی چند
Have no eye of (expectation of) favor from some animals.

پیر میخانه چه خوش گفت به دردی کش خویش
To his dreg-drinker, how well spake the Pir[2] of the wine-house,
که مگو حال دل سوخته با خامی چند
Saying: "Utter not the state of the consumed heart to some immature ones."

1-Muslims turn at prayer.
2-A Muslim saint or holy man, Pietist

January 24 - ۴ بهمن

سیل است آب دیده و هر کس که بگذرد
The water of (our) eye is a great torrent By whomsoever it passeth,
گر خود دلش ز سنگ بود هم ز جا رود
Though his heart be of stone, from place (senseless and intoxicated) it (the heart) goeth

ما را به آب دیده شب و روز ماجراست
As to the water of our eye, night and day, ours is the talk,
زان رهگذر که بر سر کویش چرا رود
Of that passage (of tears) that, at the head of His street, why it (the tear) goeth

January 25 - ۵ بهمن

تا ز میخانه و می نام و نشان خواهد بود
As long as name and trace of the tavern' (the existence of the traveller) rand of wine shall be,
سر ما خاک ره پیر مغان خواهد بود
The dust of the path of the Pir of the Magians (the murshid of love who is the King of seekers) the our head, shall be

حلقه پیر مغان از ازلم در گوش است
From eternity without beginning, the ring of (obedience of) the Pir of the Magians was in my ear
بر همانیم که بودیم و همان خواهد بود
In this way, we are as we were thus it (the ring) shall be

January 26 - ۶ بهمن

خستگان را چو طلب باشد و قوت نبود
Those shattered, when they are in search of thee (of thee) and (theirs) power is not,
گر تو بیداد کنی شرط مروت نبود
If thou vex, the condition of manliness is not.

ما جفا از تو ندیدیم و تو خود نپسندی
From thee, we experienced no tyranny and thou thyself approvest not
آن چه در مذهب ارباب طریقت نبود
What, in the Order of the Shaikh soft he Path, is not

January 27 - ۷ بهمن

می خواه و گل افشان کن از دهر چه می جویی
"Wine, demand; rose-scattering, make; from time, what seekest thou?"

این گفت سحرگه گل بلبل تو چه می گویی
Thus, at morn, to the bulbul[1] spake the rose. What sayest thou?

مسند به گلستان بر تا شاهد و ساقی را
To the rose-garden, the cushion take; so that of the lovely one and of the Saki,

لب گیری و رخ بوسی می نوشی و گل بویی
The lip, thou mayst take, and the cheek, kiss; (so that) wine thou mayst drink and the rose, smell.

January 28 - ۸ بهمن

گر من از باغ تو یک میوه بچینم چه شود
If, from thy garden, I pluck a rose, what may it be

پیش پایی به چراغ تو ببینم چه شود
(If) by thy lamp (of splendour) I see before my feet what may it

یا رب اندر کنف سایه آن سرو بلند
O Lord! (God) within the border of the shade of that lofty cypress,

گر من سوخته یک دم بنشینم چه شود
If, a moment a tease, I consumed sate, what may it be.

January 29 - ۹ بهمن

گوهر مخزن اسرار همان است که بود
Verily the jewel of the treasure of mysteries is a sit was

حقه مهر بدان مهر و نشان است که بود
With that seal and mark, the chest of (our) love is as it was.

عاشقان زمره ارباب امانت باشند
Lovers are the crowd of the Lords of deposit

لاجرم چشم گهربار همان است که بود
Doubt less, the eye, jewel-raining, is a sit was,

1- Nightingale

January 30 - بهمن ۱۰

یک دو جامم دی سحرگه اتفاق افتاده بود
In the morning-time, me the opportunity of drinking one or two cups (of manifestations of glories) had be fallen
و از لب ساقی شرابم در مذاق افتاده بود
And into my palate from the lip of the Saki (whose quality is discourse) wine delight-giving had fallen

از سر مستی دگر با شاهد عهد شباب
With the lovely one of lusty youth's time, again, through intoxication,
رجعتی می‌خواستم لیکن طلاق افتاده بود
I desired restitution of conjugal rights But divorce (from youth's time) had fallen

January 31 - بهمن ۱۱

اگر آن طایر قدسی ز درم بازآید
If, by my door, that holy bird (the true Beloved) comeback
عمر بگذشته به پیرانه سرم بازآید
To me, elderly of head, my passed life may come back.

دارم امید بر این اشک چو باران که دگر
With these my tears like rain, I hope that
برق دولت که برفت از نظرم بازآید
The lightning of fortune, that departed from my sight, may come back.

February 1 - بهمن ۱۲

دیدم به خواب خوش که به دستم پیاله بود
In a pleasant dream, I be held that in my hand, the cup was
تعبیر رفت و کار به دولت حواله بود
Interpretation passed; and, entrusted to fortune, the work was

چهل سال رنج و غصه کشیدیم و عاقبت
Forty years I endured trouble and vexation (in love's path) In the end,
تدبیر ما به دست شراب دوساله بود
In the power of wine, two years of age (the glorious Kuran, wherein I find every delight I sought) the deliberation of it was.

February 2 - ۱۳ بهمن

هرگزم نقش تو از لوح دل و جان نرود
From the tablet of my heart and soul, Thy image, ever goeth not
هرگز از یاد من آن سرو خرامان نرود
From my recollection, that proudly moving cypress ever goeth not

از دماغ من سرگشته خیال دهنت
(O true Beloved) From my distraught brain, the image of Thy cheek
به جفای فلک و غصه دوران نرود
By the sky's violence and time's wrath, goeth not

February 3 - ۱۴ بهمن

بخت از دهان دوست نشانم نمی‌دهد
Trace of the (true) Beloved's mouth, fortune giveth me not.
دولت خبر ز راز نهانم نمی‌دهد
News of the hidden mystery, fortune giveth me not

از بهر بوسه‌ای ز لبش جان همی‌دهم
For a kiss from His lip, I surrender my life
اینم همی‌ستاند و آنم نمی‌دهد
This (my life) He taketh not; and that (the kiss) He giveth me not

February 4 - ۱۵ بهمن

حدیث از مطرب و می گو و راز دهر کمتر جو
The tale of minstrel and of wine (of Love) utter; little seek the mystery of time;
که کس نگشود و نگشاید به حکمت این معما را
For this mystery, none solved by skill (thought and knowledge); and shall not solve.

غزل گفتی و در سفتی بیا و خوش بخوان حافظ
Thou utteredest a ghazal[1]; and threadedest pearls (of verse). Hafez! come and sweetly sing
که بر نظم تو افشاند فلک عقد ثریا را
That, on thy verse, the sky may scatter (in thanks) the cluster of the Pleiades.

1-Sonnet

February 5 - ۱۶ بهمن

بنمای رخ که خلق واله شوند و حیران
Show thy (lovely) face, a whole people go lamenting and wailing (in love for thee)

بگشای لب که فریاد از مرد و زن برآید
Open thy lip (to speak) from man and woman, cry cometh forth

جان بر لب است و حسرت در دل که از لبانش
The soul is on the lip (ready to depart) and vexation in the heart. For, from this mouth,

نگرفته هیچ کامی جان از بدن برآید
Not a single desire taken, from the body, the soul cometh forth.

February 6 - ۱۷ بهمن

گفتم غم تو دارم گفت غمت سر آید
To (the true Beloved) I said: "Grief for Thee, I have." He said: "To an end (when union is attained) thy grief cometh"

گفتم که ماه من شو گفتا اگر برآید
I spake saying: "Be my moon." (make luminous like the moon my eye and bosom). He said (I will be thy moon) "if forth the chance cometh"

گفتم ز مهرورزان رسم وفا بیاموز
I said: "From kind ones (lovers) learn the usage of fidelity Seldom cometh."

گفتا ز خوبرویان این کار کمتر آید
He said: "From those moon of face (lovely women) this work of fidelity Seldom cometh."

February 7 - ۱۸ بهمن

گر رود از پی خوبان دل من معذور است
If for the pursuit of lovely ones, my heart goeth, 'tis excusable

درد دارد چه کند کز پی درمان نرود
It hath (love's) pain. What may it do if, for remedy-sake, it goeth not?

هر که خواهد که چو حافظ نشود سرگردان
Whoever head-be wildered like Hafiz, wisheth not to become

دل به خوبان ندهد و از پی ایشان نرود
Giveth not his heart to lovely ones and, in pursuit of them, goeth not

February 8 - بهمن ۱۹

خوشا دلی که مدام از پی نظر نرود
O happy that heart that, ever, after the illusory goeth not,
به هر درش که بخوانند بی خبر نرود
To every door where to they call him not, without notice (invitation) he goeth not

طمع در آن لب شیرین نکردنم اولی
Best for me, not to set desire upon that sweet lip
ولی چگونه مگس از پی شکر نرود
But after sugar, 'what kind of fly goeth not

February 9 - بهمن ۲۰

گر چه بر واعظ شهر این سخن آسان نشود
Although to the city-admonisher, easy this matter becometh not
تا ریا ورزد و سالوس مسلمان نشود
So long as hypocrisy and deceit, hepractiseth, Musulman, he becometh not

رندی آموز و کرم کن که نه چندان هنر است
Learn profligacy and practise liberality For not such a great matter is it,
حیوانی که ننوشد می و انسان نشود
That wine, a mere animal drinketh not and man becometh not

February 10 - بهمن ۲۱

رواق منظر چشم من آشیانه توست
(O true Beloved) The chamber of vision of my eye is the dwelling of Thine:
کرم نما و فرود آ که خانه خانۀ توست
Show courtesy, and alight, for this house is the House of Thine.

دلت به وصل گل ای بلبل صبا خوش باد
O nightingale! (the perfect murshid) glad of heart be, in union with the rosethe true Beloved.
که در چمن همه گلبانگ عاشقانه توست
For, in the sward (the world), the amorous warbling (the melody of utterance of divine truths) all is thine.

February 11 - ۲۲ بهمن

یاد باد آن که نهانت نظری با ما بود
Be memory of that time (0 true Beloved) when towards us Thy exceeding glance (of mercy) was.

رقم مهر تو بر چهره ما پیدا بود
(When) evident in our face, the writing of Thy love (mercy) was.

یاد باد آن که چو چشمت به عتابم می‌کشت
Be memory of that time when, me with reproach, Thy eye slew

معجز عیسویت در لب شکرخا بود
(When) in Thy lip, sugar-devouring, the miracle of Isa (life-giving) was.

February 12 - ۲۳ بهمن

اگر به باده مشکین دلم کشد شاید
If the heart draw me to musky wine, it be fitteth

که بوی خیر ز زهد ریا نمی‌آید
For, from austerity and hypocrisy, the perfume of goodness cometh not.

جهانیان همه گر منع من کنند از عشق
If all the people of the world forbid me love,

من آن کنم که خداوندگار فرماید
(Yet) that which the Lord commandeth, I shall do.

February 13 - ۲۴ بهمن

ساقی و مطرب و می جمله مهیاست ولی
The cup, and the minstrel, and the rose, all are ready.

عیش بی یار مهیا نشود یار کجاست
But, ease without the Beloved is not attainable. The Beloved is where?

حافظ از باد خزان در چمن دهر مرنج
Hafez! grieve not of (cruel) the autumn wind (which bloweth) in the sward of the world:

فکر معقول بفرما گل بی خار کجاست
Exercise reasonable thought. The rose (time) without the thorn (the autumn wind) is where?

February 14 - ۲۵ بهمن

بر سر آنم که گر ز دست برآید
In desire of that I am that, if, forth from my hand, it come,
دست به کاری زنم که غصه سر آید
I may fix my hand upon a work such that the end of grief may come.

خلوت دل نیست جای صحبت اضداد
The plain of vision of the heart is not a place of society of opponents
دیو چو بیرون رود فرشته درآید
When the demon goeth out, the angel within may come.

February 15 - ۲۶ بهمن

خون شد دلم به یاد تو هر گه که در چمن
In memory of thee, blood become my heart, whenever, in the sward,
بند قبای غنچه گل می‌گشاد باد
The fastening of the rose-bud's coat, loosed the wind.

از دست رفته بود وجود ضعیف من
From my hand, had gone my feeble existence:
صبحم به بوی وصل تو جان بازداد باد
In the morning, by the perfume of thy tress, gave back life, the wind.

February 16 - ۲۷ بهمن

واعظان کاین جلوه در محراب و منبر می‌کنند
The (outward) admonishers who, in the prayer-arch and the pulpit, grandeur (of exhortation) make,
چون به خلوت می‌روند آن کار دیگر می‌کنند
When into their chamber they go, that work of another kind they make.

مشکلی دارم ز دانشمند مجلس بازپرس
A difficulty, I have. Ask the wisp ones of the assembly, (those ordering penitence)
توبه فرمایان چرا خود توبه کمتر می‌کنند
Why those ordering penitence, themselves penitence seldom make?

February 17 - ۲۸ بهمن

چو دست بر سر زلفش زنم به تاب رود
When I place my hand on the tip of His tress, in wrath He goeth
ور آشتی طلبم با سر عتاب رود
If I seek concord, with a head (full) of rebuke, He goeth
چو ماه نو ره بیچارگان نظاره
Like the new moon, helpless spectators
زند به گوشه ابرو و در نقاب رود
Heat tack eth with the corner of the eye-brow and, into the veil, goeth

February 18 - ۲۹ بهمن

زهی خجسته زمانی که یار بازآید
O how happy the time when the Beloved cometh back.
به کام غمزدگان غمگسار بازآید
When to the desire of the grief-stricken, the grief-consoler cometh back
به پیش خیل خیالش کشیدم ابلق چشم
Before the king of his fancy, the black and the white of the eye, I extended,
بدان امید که آن شهسوار بازآید
In that hope that that imperial horseman might comeback.

February 19 - ۳۰ بهمن

گر بود عمر به میخانه رسم بار دگر
If life were, to the wine-house, I would go another time:
بجز از خدمت رندان نکنم کار دگر
Save the service of profligates, I would do no other work.
خرم آن روز که با دیده گریان بروم
Happy that day, when, with weeping eye, I go
تا زنم آب در میکده یک بار دگر
So that, on the wine-house door, water (of tears) I may dash another time

فصل زمستان
(Winter)

اسفند

March

February 20 - اسفند ۱

نصیحتی کنمت بشنو و بهانه مگیر
A piece of advice, I make thee listen make no excuse
هر آن چه ناصح مشفق بگویدت بپذیر
Whatever the kind admonisher saith to thee, accept.

ز وصل روی جوانان تمتعی بردار
With those of youthful face, the enjoyment of union take up
که در کمینگه عمر است مکر عالم پیر
For, in ambush of life, is the deceit of the old world.

February 21 - اسفند ۲

باغبانا ز خزان بی‌خبرت می‌بینم
O gardener! (outward worshipper) careless of the autumn, (the resurrection, day) I behold thee:
آه از آن روز که بادت گل رعنا ببرد
Alas! that day when thy beautiful rose (of desire) the wind of death taketh.

رهزن دهر نخفته‌ست مشو ایمن از او
Time's highwayman (Shaitan) hath not slept. Of him, be not secure,
اگر امروز نبرده‌ست که فردا ببرد
If thee, he hath not taken today. For, to-morrow, thee he taketh.

February 22 - اسفند ۳

ای صبا نکهتی از خاک ره یار بیار
O breeze from the dust of the (true) Beloved's path, a perfume bring:
ببر اندوه دل و مژده دلدار بیار
My heart's grief, take; glad tidings of the heart-possessor bring.

نکته‌ای روح فزا از دهن دوست بگو
(O breeze) From the (true) Beloved's mouth, a soul-expanding subtlety utter
نامه‌ای خوش خبر از عالم اسرار بیار
From the world of mysteries, a letter of pleasant news bring.

February 23 - ۴ اسفند

به لب رسید مرا جان و برنیامد کام
(Ready to depart) My soul reached the lip and desire was not accomplished
به سر رسید امید و طلب به سر نرسید
To an end, reached my hope; to an end, reached (fulfilment) not my desire

ز شوق روی تو حافظ نوشت حرفی چند
Some words, through desire of thy face, Hafiz wrote.
بخوان ز نظمش و در گوش کن چو مروارید
In his verse, read (the pearls) and. like pearls, put (the verse) in thy ear.

February 24 - ۵ اسفند

قحط جود است آبروی خود نمی‌باید فروخت
'Tis the drought of liberality it is not proper to sell my own honour
باده و گل از بهای خرقه می‌باید خرید
For the price of the Khirka, wine and the rose it is proper to buy.

گویا خواهد گشود از دولتم کاری که دوش
From my fortune, he will probably unfold a great work. For, last night,
من همی‌کردم دعا و صبح صادق می‌دمید
I prayed, and the dawn of creation dawned.

February 25 - ۶ اسفند

سرو چمان من چرا میل چمن نمی‌کند
Inclination for the sward, the cypress of my sward, (the Beloved) wberefore maketh not?
همدم گل نمی‌شود یاد سمن نمی‌کند
The fellow-companion of the rose, (wherefore) becometh not? Memory of the lily (wherefore) maketh not?

دی گله‌ای ز طره‌اش کردم و از سر فسوس
(To the Beloved) I complained last night of (the tyranny of) His tress. By way of regret
گفت که این سیاه کج گوش به من نمی‌کند
He spake saying to me, the ear (of attention) this black curly (tress) maketh not.

February 26 - ۷ اسفند

خرقه زهد و جام می گر چه نه درخور همند
Though not fitted matched together are the Khirka[1] of austerity, and the cup of wine,
این همه نقش می‌زنم از جهت رضای تو
All this picture, I paint trick I play for the sake of the will of Thine

شور شراب عشق تو آن نفسم رود ز سر
Goeth from my head, wine's clamouring (and) love's (consuming) at that moment
کاین سر پرهوس شود خاک در سرای تو
When this head full of passion becometh the dust of the door of the ab ode of Thine.

February 27 - ۸ اسفند

معاشران ز حریف شبانه یاد آرید
O dear friends of the friend of the night, -bring ye to mind
حقوق بندگی مخلصانه یاد آرید
The duties of since reservice, bring ye to mind.

به وقت سرخوشی از آه و ناله عشاق
At intoxication's time, of the weeping and the wailing of lovers,
به صوت و نغمه چنگ و چغانه یاد آرید
To the sound (of) the melody of the harp and of the cymbal, bring ye to mind.

February 28 - ۹ اسفند

اوقات خوش آن بود که با دوست به سر رفت
Happy were those times which passed with the friend
باق همه بی‌حاصلی و بی‌خبری بود
All without result and without knowledge, the rest was

خوش بود لب آب و گل و سبزه و نسرین
Sweet was the marge of the water, and the rose and the verdure. But
افسوس که آن گنج روان رهگذری بود
Alas that moving treasure, away-farer was.

1-Cloak

March 1 - ۱۰ اسفند

در آرزوی خاک در یار سوختیم
In desire of the dust of the Friend's path, I consumed,
یاد آور ای صبا که نکردی حمایتی
O morning breeze bring to mind that even a little protection thou gavest not.

ای دل به هرزه دانش و عمرت به باد رفت
O heart in absurd knowledge (thou wast) and, (from the hand) life passed
صد مایه داشتی و نکردی کفایتی
A hundred sources (of capital) thou hadst and a sufficiency, thou madest not.

March 2 - ۱۱ اسفند

اگر رفیق شفیقی درست پیمان باش
If thou be the compassionate friend, true of covenant, be:
حریف خانه و گرمابه و گلستان باش
The companion of the closet (in grief) and of the hot bath and of the rose-garden (in ease) be

شکنج زلف پریشان به دست باد مده
To the power of wine, the curl of thy dishevelled tress give not (so that its perfume may not agitate lovers)
مگو که خاطر عشاق گو پریشان باش
Speak not saying Say, lovers' hearts agitated be

March 3 - ۱۲ اسفند

بکش جفای رقیبان مدام و جور حسود
The tyranny of the watchers, ever endure; (happy of heart, be);
که سهل باشد اگر یار مهربان داری
For' tis easy, if the kind Beloved thou hast.

به وصل دوست گرت دست می‌دهد یک دم
If, one moment, to thy hand, union with the Friend reacheth,
برو که هر چه مراد است در جهان داری
Go (do thy work) For, whatever desire is in the world, thou hast.

March 4 - ۴ اسفند ۱۳

چمن خوش است و هوا دلکش است و می بی‌غش
Pleasant is the sward heart-alluring is the air pure is the wine
کنون بجز دل خوش هیچ در نمی‌باید
Now, save the joyous heart, naught is wanting.

جمیله‌ایست عروس جهان ولی هش دار
Beautiful is the bride of the world. But keep sense
که این مخدره در عقد کس نمی‌آید
For, into no one's bond, comethth is young maiden.

March 5 - ۵ اسفند ۱۴

دولت پیر مغان باد که باقی سهل است
Be the fortune (wherein is no decline) of the Pir of the Magians, because (the travelling of) the rest is easy
دیگری گو برو و نام من از یاد ببر
((If) another (go) say Go and (out) from thy memory (for easy is this) our name, take.

سعی نابرده در این راه به جایی نرسی
In this path (of divine knowledge) effort not borne, (thou) reachest not to place (of rank)
مزد اگر می‌طلبی طاعت استاد ببر
If thou see k the reward, the service of the teacher (the murshid) take.

March 6 - ۶ اسفند ۱۵

بوی خوش تو هر که ز باد صبا شنید
From the morning-breeze, thy pleasant perfume, who perceived
از یار آشنا سخن آشنا شنید
From the dear friend (the breeze) he (true) Beloved's speech (who) heard.

ای شاه حسن چشم به حال گدا فکن
O King of beauty (the true Beloved) cast Thy eye (of mercy) on the state of the beggar (Thy lover)
کاین گوش بس حکایت شاه و گدا شنید
For, many a tale of the King (beggar,-cherishing) and of the beggar, this ear heard

140

۱۶ اسفند - March 7

صبر بر جور رقیبت چه کنم گر نکنم

If, as to the watcher's tyranny patience I exercise not, what may I do

عاشقان را نبود چاره بجز مسکینی

To wretched lovers, is no remedy save wretchedness.

باد صبحی به هوایت ز گلستان برخاست

From the rose-garden, a rose a morning breeze in desire of thee

که تو خوشتر ز گل و تازه‌تر از نسرینی

For, more pleasant than the red rose and more fresh than the wild white rose, thou art.

۱۷ اسفند - March 8

صبا ز منزل جانان گذر دریغ مدار

O breeze (murshid) thy passing by the dwelling of the (true) Beloved, keep not back

وز او به عاشق بی‌دل خبر دریغ مدار

For the wretched lover (Hafiz) news of Him (the true Beloved) keep not back

به شکر آن که شکفتی به کام بخت ای گل

O rose in thanks that, to thy heart's desire, thou blossomedest,

نسیم وصل ز مرغ سحر دریغ مدار

From the bird of the morning (the nightingale) the breeze of union keep not back

۱۸ اسفند - March 9

روی بنمای و وجود خودم از یاد ببر

(O beloved) display thy face and my existence from my mind take

خرمن سوختگان را همه گو باد ببر

(And) the harvest of those consumed (lovers), say O wind all take

ما چو دادیم دل و دیده به طوفان بلا

When to the deluge of calamity, we gave our heart and eye,

گو بیا سیل غم و خانه ز بنیاد ببر

Say: Come grief's torrent, and up, from its foundation, our house take.

March 10 - اسفند ۱۹

یار مفروش به دنیا که بسی سود نکرد
The (true) Beloved, sell not for the world (and in the world's attachments be not foot – bound) For, much, it profited not
آن که یوسف به زر ناسره بفروخته بود
That one who, for base gold, Yusuf[1], had sold.

گفت و خوش گفت برو خرقه بسوزان حافظ
He spake, and sweetly spake Hafiz go and (burn) the Khirka[2]
یا رب این قلب شناسی ز که آموخته بود
O Lord! from whom, this (power of) base-coin recognising (is it that) He had learned.

March 11 - اسفند ۲۰

نفس برآمد و کام از تو بر نمی‌آید
The breath (of life) is sued; and forth from thee, my desire (of union) cometh not
فغان که بخت من از خواب در نمی‌آید
Clamour for, forth from sleep, my fortune cometh not.

صبا به چشم من انداخت خاکی از کویش
Into my eye, the breeze cast a little dust from His street
که آب زندگیم در نظر نمی‌آید
For, into my vision, the water of life cometh not.

March 12 - اسفند ۲۱

ای صبا نکهتی از کوی فلانی به من آر
O breeze from such a one's street, me, a perfume bring.
زار و بیمار غمم راحت جانی به من آر
Weeping and sad of grief, I am me, ease of soul, bring:

قلب بی‌حاصل ما را بزن اکسیر مراد
For our profit less heart, strike out the elixir of purpose
یعنی از خاک در دوست نشانی به من آر
That is From the dust of the Beloved's door (which is indeed an elixir) me, a trace bring.

1-Name of prophet
2-Cloak

March 13 - اسفند ۲۲

اگر ز مردم هشیاری ای نصیحتگو
O counsel-utterer if (the crowd of) men of sense, thou be,
سخن به خاک میفکن چرا که من مستم
The dust, cast not thy speech (of counsel) for (counsel is useless) intoxicated I am.

چگونه سر ز خجالت برآورم بر دوست
Before the Friend (God) my head forth from shame how may I bring,
که خدمتی به سزا برنیامد از دستم
When, from my hand, a worthy service issueth not

March 14 - اسفند ۲۳

هزار دشمنم ار می‌کنند قصد هلاک
If design for my destruction, thousands of enemies (Shaitans, intent upon leading one astray) make
گرم تو دوستی از دشمنان ندارم باک
If thou (O perfect murshid) be my friend (and aider) and of enemies, I have no fear

مرا امید وصال تو زنده می‌دارد
Me, hope of union with Thee keepeth alive
و گر نه هر دمم از هجر توست بیم هلاک
If not, from separation from Thee a hundred ways, fear of destruction is (mine)

March 15 - اسفند ۲۴

من نمی‌یابم مجال ای دوستان
O friends power (of union with Him) I gain not,
گر چه دارد او جمالی بس جمیل
For the reason that exceedingly beauteous beauty, He hath.

پای ما لنگ است و منزل بس دراز
Lame is our foot; (and far distant, is) the stage (like Paradise)
دست ما کوتاه و خرما بر نخیل
Short, is our hand and on the (lofty inaccessible) date-tree, the date.

March 16 - ۲۵ اسفند

دست از طلب ندارم تا کام من برآید
From desire (of the beloved) I restrain not my hand until my desire cometh forth
یا تن رسد به جانان یا جان ز تن برآید
Either to the beloved, my body reacheth or, from the body, my soul cometh forth.
بگشای تربتم را بعد از وفات و بنگر
(O beloved) after my death, open my tomb and be hold
کز آتش درونم دود از کفن برآید
From the fire of my heart, smoke from the shroud cometh forth.

March 17 - ۲۶ اسفند

چو بر در تو من بی‌نوای بی زر و زور
When, at Thy door, without resource, without gold or force,
به هیچ باب ندارم ره خروج و دخول
I have, in no way, the path of egress or of ingress.
کجا روم چه کنم چاره از کجا جویم
I go where I do what (I am) how Remedy, (I make what),
که گشته‌ام ز غم و جور روزگار ملول
For, from grief of time's violence, sorely vexed I am become.

March 18 - ۲۷ اسفند

چو بشنوی سخن اهل دل مگو که خطاست
O Heart-ravisher! thou art not a speech-recognizer. Here, the fault is:
سخن شناس نه‌ای جان من خطا این جاست
When thou hearest the speech of people of heart speak not saying: "A fault it is."
سرم به دنیی و عقبی فرو نمی‌آید
Neither to this world, nor to the next world, boweth my head (filled with great ideas)
تبارک الله از این فتنه‌ها که در سر ماست
Blessed be God! for this tumult that, in our head, is.

March 19 - ۲۸ اسفند

گر چه گردآلود فقرم شرم باد از همتم
Dust-stained with poverty though I be, of my spirit, be shame,

گر به آب چشمه خورشید دامن تر کنم
If, with the water (of liberality) of the sun's fountain, my skirt wet I make.

عاشقان را گر در آتش می‌پسندد لطف دوست
If the Friend's grace approve (casting) of lovers into the fire (of hell)

تنگ چشمم گر نظر در چشمه کوثر کنم
Closed of eye, I am (even) if, on the fountain of Kausar[1], glance I make

March 20 - ۲۹ اسفند

رسید مژده که آمد بهار و سبزه دمید
Arrived the glad news that come hath spring; and up-sprung the verdure

وظیفه گر برسد مصرفش گل است و نبید
If the allowance arrive, its expenditure will be the rose and wine

صفیر مرغ برآمد بط شراب کجاست
Ascendeth the piping of the bird. The leathern flagon of wine is where.

فغان فتاد به بلبل نقاب گل که کشید
Falleth clamour upon the bulbuls the rose's veil, who drew back.

1-It is a spring in heaven

حافظ شیرازی

خواجه شمس‌الدّین محمّد شیرازی متخلص به "حافظ" مشهور به لِسانُ الْغِیْب، تَرجُمانُ الْاَسرار، بلبل شیراز، خواجه عرفان، کاشف الحقایق، مجذوب سالک، غزل سرای بزرگ و از خداوندان شعر و ادب پارسی سده ی هشتم هجری قمری شیراز است. او در دوران جوانی بر تمام علوم مذهبی و ادبی تسلط یافت و قرآن را حفظ نمود و در دهه بیست زندگی به یکی از مشاهیر علم و ادب دیار خود تبدل شد.

در دوران امارات شاه شیخ ابواسحاق به دربار راه پیدا کرده و علاوه بر شاه اسحاق در دربار شاهان آل مظفر به نام شاه مبارزالدین، شاه شجاع، شاه منصور و شاه یحیی راه داشته است.

دیوان اشعار او شامل غزلیات و چند قصیده، چند مثنوی، قطعات، رباعیات است. موضوع اشعار او بیشتر عرفانی و با موضوع وحدت وجود می باشد نوآوری اصلی حافظ در تک بیت های درخشان، مستقل و خوش مضمون است. موضوع غزل وصف معشوق، می، و مغازله است و غزل سرایی را باید هنری دانست ادبی، که درخور سرود و غنا و ترانه پردازی است. موضوع اشعار حافظ بسیار متنوع بوده و از شعرهای او در موسیقی سنتی ایرانی، هنرهای تجسمی و خوشنویسی استفاده می شود.

از آن جایی که حافظ تنها در لحظاتی که خاص و الهام بخش بود به سرودن اشعارش می پرداخت، به طور متوسط در هر سال فقط ۱۰ غزل و دیوان خود را در طول ۵۰ سال سروده و تمرکز او خلق اثری شایسته مقام واقعی معشوق بوده است.

تعداد نسخه های خطّی ساده یا تذهیب شده آن در کتابخانه های ایران، افغانستان، هند، پاکستان، ترکیه و حتی کشورهای غربی دیگری از هر دیوان فارسی بیشتر است. تاکنون بیش از چهارصد بار به اشکال مختلف به زبان فارسی و به چندین زبان از جمله انگلیسی، فرانسوی، روسی، عربی، اردو، پنجابی، سندی، هندی، پشتو و بلوچی در دنیا به چاپ رسیده است.

وی به سال ۷۹۲ هجری قمری در شیراز درگذشت. آرامگاه او در شهر شیراز و در منطقهٔ حافظیه، زیارتگاه صاحب‌نظران و عاشقان شعر و ادب پارسی است. هر ساله در تاریخ بیستم مهرماه مراسم بزرگداشت حافظ در محل آرامگاه او در شیراز با حضور پژوهشگران ایرانی و خارجی برگزار می شود.

سالی با حافظ

با ترجمه انگلیسی:
Henry Wilberforce Clarke

گردآوری:
حمید اسلامیان

Printed in Great Britain
by Amazon